Christ Above Culture

A Gospel-Centered Vision for Racial Harmony

Sherard Burns

A ROCC BOOKS publication

ROCC BOOKS is the publishing ministry of Renewing Our Culture for Christ (ROCC). The mission of ROCC is to bring reformation and renewal to the African American church and community. Through the various ministries of ROCC the aim is to *Touch hearts, Transform lives, and Shape the future.*

RENEWING OUR CULTURE FOR CHRIST

Touching hearts, Transforming lives, Shaping the future

Sermon To Book
www.sermontobook.com

Christ Above Culture / Sherard Burns
ISBN-13: 9780692709702
ISBN-10: 0692709703

May the Lord use this imperfect book to help in the following ways:

To communicate – His perfect truth

To encourage – His achieved harmony

To build – His beloved Church.

May the churches we leave behind be a beautiful manifestation of the glory of God for the coming generations of Christianity.

CONTENTS

A Man Between Cultures
My Journey in Racial Harmony

I was nineteen. I was a student at Tuskegee University in Tuskegee, Alabama, and I was at the dawn of entering into the ministry. In the town, there were still remnants of the racial divide that was so explosively evident some years earlier in another city, Selma. I was young, and in many ways I remained a bit naive about race relations and even more so about the Bible's teaching regarding them. Still, I knew that the hidden tensions of division in 1990 were somehow a contradiction to the gospel. I felt the error but was unaware of how to think about the matter, much less speak to it.

I remember listening to a well-known radio preacher begin to address the issue that he called "racial reconciliation." I listened with eagerness and awe as he spoke about racial division as not a thing of the past but a current problem in the world as well as in the church! It was a beautiful word spoken that day to my soul. It was beautiful not because it validated the existence of racial division in the church but because it gave validity to what I was feeling regarding the tensions in Tuskegee. It also provided the beginnings of the biblical and theological content for what would form the essence of my life and ministry.

God sovereignly spoke to me in that moment. I was not only called to a specific ministry, I believed, but I was personally challenged regarding the issue in my own heart and life. While I was transformed on that day, a problem was manifested in my own life. I was a young African American man who had gone to an all-black church since I was thirteen. At the time of hearing the preacher on the radio, I was serving as an associate pastor at a small church in Tuskegee, Alabama, which was also all black. Was my own existence proof of the divide? I was never moved to ask that question until that day when the Lord massively changed my thinking and life as a minister of the gospel.

Then came Promise Keepers. From the initial stirring when I was nineteen, God began the wave of Promise Keepers events that launched the entire church into an awakening about the role and impact of racial division in the church as well as the need for change. While much about the Promise Keepers approach has been questioned, it is doubtful that any other event or movement has opened the eyes of so many to this dilemma—some of whom had never given much thought to it before. One of the handicaps of the movement, however, was its popularization of racial reconciliation without a consistent, theological track for sustaining it.

Men would gather and exchange nice and sincere expressions of commitment to fight against the racial divide. Men cried on the bus and endeavored to keep meeting when they returned home. The sad reality was that I never saw those men again, and this, I add, is to my own shame. What I began to discover at this point was that mere sentimentality is not enough to battle this destructive expression in the church, not to mention in our own lives and affections. In small and untested ways, I began to recognize that something more was needed, though I was unable fully to articulate my burden.

In the fall of 1995, another significant move of God came into my life that would forever change not only my view of salvation but also the way I understood events in history. In that season, the Lord opened my eyes to the radical and all-encompassing nature of His sovereignty through the doctrines of grace. This changed the way I viewed His character, ways, and purposes in all of life, including my own.

I was then twenty-three and was pastoring a small church in Lochapoka, Alabama. I had been convinced of expositional preaching through the ministry of John MacArthur and had begun preaching through the book of Ephesians. I was struck by the awesome reality that God had chosen me from the foundation of the world, before I was born (Ephesians 1:4). God had raised me up together with Christ and seated me with Him in the heavenly places (Ephesians 2:6). This wonderful truth caused me to understand that the faith I possessed was actually a gift from God, established before the world began. I was His because I had been *chosen*.

I began to preach this as a wonderful new discovery. However, as Solomon tells us, "there is nothing new under the sun" (Ecclesiastes 1:9). I would later come to see that this was nothing new at all. It was not the invention of my own mind; rather, it was the theology expressed in the Protestant Reformation by men like Martin Luther and John Calvin. I would come to see that God was sovereign (in full control) not only in the redemption of man but also in every single event in all of history. A new world was opened to me. This new theological outlook provided the foundation that would solidify my entire worldview.

In that season of my life, God became God. I had loved Him and served Him as such, but when my eyes were opened to the reality that all things are under His control, it was as if someone had opened the blinds all the way and exposed me to the fullness of the sun! I was then prepared to think biblically about the racial divisions that confronted the church.

What I found was an understanding of how the gospel stands central in all aspects of life. It seemed as if I had been spiritually reborn and all that I could do was seek and devour the Bible and other good books that gave deeper insight into what I had discovered. I had thought about the possibility of attending seminary before, but now it was nonnegotiable. My new passion led me to desire more knowledge of this theology. In the providence of God, I was able to attend seminary and receive training that further illuminated my understanding and gave clarity to my life and ministry. This seminary was predominantly white.

It was here that I was forced to consider how racial harmony should and could be fleshed out in a Christ- and gospel-centered way. I was not physically forced but intellectually since the seminary was almost exclusively white. I was in a situation where I could either let my blackness dominate my Christianity or use this as an opportunity to allow my life to reflect the gospel in racial unity.

I found seminary to be the most challenging place, racially speaking, I had ever been. It was not that anyone said or did anything that made it so, but it was here that I found the powerful influence that culture had on others and would soon discover its influence on me.

I was working through all kinds of issues at this point. I was an African American who embraced a theology that, at the time, I thought was exclusively believed by whites. This factor caused me to question things in a way I stand ashamed of to this day. I questioned the usefulness of the black church. In anger, I wondered why I was never taught such great and soul-transforming biblical theology.

I wondered why the black churches and pastors seemed to focus so much on the emotional when there was this wealth of theological instruction that laid men before the beauty and greatness of God. White music, I was beginning to believe, was the better music because it highlighted the great doctrines of the Bible and spoke to the truth of who God is. Black music was good for emotional uplifting, but because it was too emotional and did not give enough biblical content, it should be considered entertainment and not worship. This is what I thought at that young age.

The disastrous framework that guided my thinking in those days can be summed up in these words: The white expression of Christianity is right, and the black expression of Christianity is deficient. I am well aware that such thinking is erroneous, but it seemed to me at the time that everything that was theologically correct had "white" attached to it. Added to this perception was the reality that very few blacks supported my seminary efforts while a white couple, Jay and Martha Tolar, who had only recently met me, decided that they would pay for the entirety of my seminary education.

So much was warring in my mind in those days, and looking back, I see that my own thinking had been infected by an ungodly perception of right and wrong as well as the determination of what is biblical or unbiblical. I was in a darkness I could not perceive.

These things shaped my faulty rationale about sound theology and its relation to the black and white church. I felt that not only did black pastors not teach me these great truths but they would not even support me in furthering my biblical education. These realities, however dark the days had been, birthed a passion in my soul to see the doctrines of grace introduced to the African American church. This passion led to another significant event: the formation of The Black Alliance for Reformed Theology (BART).

Recognizing the dearth of solid theological teaching and preaching in the black church and desiring to be an agent of change, I, along with a close friend, formed a web ministry that would reach out and begin to build a coalition of African American reformed men and women across the country. This not only awakened us to mass numbers of like-minded African Americans across the country but also began a necessary shift in my mind and affections concerning the black church. I learned that God always has His remnant, and this gave tremendous joy and encouragement to my heart. It was also a necessary experience and preparation for what was about to come.

White people were comfortable with me. I felt like this was the mission of racial harmony. However, what I began to see was that their comfort around me gave them permission, they assumed, to speak freely. Many began to tell me everything that was wrong with the black church because my disposition and rhetoric made them think that I felt the same way. Something was changing within me in ways they could not know. I had found black men and women who loved and were teaching sound doctrine, and because of this my thoughts of the black church were being informed.

When negative words were spoken about the black church, I began to feel that they were talking about "my" people. One man even suggested that a white church rather than a black church would be a better fit for me because of the fact that I was receiving formal theological training. My soul and my mind had had enough. I began to look back over my experiences in the black church as well as its history, now with the cultural edges cut off. I was seeing more clearly than ever before.

In His sovereignty, the Lord had led me through a mental and emotional wilderness and was giving shape to the ministry He had given me. In His merciful purpose for my life, He delivered me from a mindset that would have been destructive to racial unity. Sitting where I am now, I see the significance of that turning point in a way I could not see it then.

Upon further reflection, I understand that what God did in my life was necessary for me not only to love this reality of racial harmony but also to be able to talk about it with a kind of cultural objectivity. God sovereignly moved me away from my black-church cultural experience so that I could look back on it with objectivity instead of embracing it all simply because it was "black." This allowed me to vet it in order to determine what was biblical in it. The same was true with respect to the white church. God was calling me away from my culture so I could assess its positive and negative aspects.

This helped me to see what was wrong in the black church—that which did not promote healthy, biblical thinking and living—as well as the positives that I had neglected because my mind was clouded by the dominant culture's perception of reality. I no longer thought that the black church was exclusively wrong and the white church was exclusively right. Each was right at times and wrong at others. Both, however, had value.

I became a man between cultures. I was black, but I became convinced that Christian theology must govern my blackness; it must give shape to how I understand, interpret, and express my human, God-given culture. I was not ashamed of being black, but I was scared, and still am, of being black *before* I am Christian. Culture is God's gift. Therefore, we should not understand it outside of His ownership and understanding of it.

I became acutely aware that I was no longer a black preacher to the black church. I was a preacher of the gospel to the church of Jesus Christ. The plan of God for the ministry He had given me was not to be understood as exclusive to one culture but to one community made up of different cultures—the church. With this conviction and calling, I felt as if I could rebuke "whiteness" and "blackness" without rebuking white and black brothers and sisters in Christ. I felt able to call things as they were—at least as I saw them—because I knew that I was not being driven by culture but, I trust and pray, by the Bible.

I am not suggesting that there were no cultural presuppositions in my heart, but I can honestly say that if they were there, I was unconscious of it. I had done things and said things out of anger, but for the most part, when I spoke about this issue, I felt convincingly biblical and free of cultural presumptions.

That I was living between cultures came home to me when one of my professors told me that one reason why some of the whites at the seminary did not like me (I was unaware of this) was because, as he put it, I could move in and out of both cultures with an ease that they resented. I am not certain of how true that was, but I learned from his statement that moving along these lines of racial harmony demands that one live between cultures and seek to saturate oneself in the culture of Christ.

I do not want to sound as if I have achieved because I certainly have not. In recent years, I have found myself on the opposite end of my own teaching. Having been called to come on staff at a predominantly white church shortly after my seminary days, my commitment to racial harmony was thoroughly challenged. The difficulty did not have to do with what people said or did but with the tension of being in a predominantly white church and struggling with how to fit. This shook me because until this point, I had felt cool, calm, and collected on this issue. I felt like I could go with the best of them, but this was different.

For instance, while I was standing in the hallway, waiting to be interviewed by the elders, a lady asked, "Are you the janitor?" On another occasion, an elderly lady asked whether or not "negro" or "colored" was the best way to describe "my people." This was an entirely new ball game. There were blacks who demanded more visible expressions of racial harmony and some whites who asked me questions about the black community as if I were the leader of the whole of black America!

Then there were those who loved the issue but were angry at my vision for racial harmony, saying that it was too programmatic and not strong enough in challenging the dominant culture's racism. These expressions were not the presence of racial division (though it was there) as much as reflections of the deep wounds that were the results of overt racism.

With all of this, however, there were a host of wonderful people who encouraged me along the way. The only problem was that their voices seemed to be muted by the negatives. I remember feeling like quitting and saying, "They can have this racial harmony stuff." Everything about what I taught—forgetting and remembering, loving difficult people—was challenged in a way that I had never experienced before. I found that all of my talking about racial harmony was theoretical and couched in artificial contexts with little action. Now God was asking me through a series of circumstances, "Do you truly believe this?"

With my faith shaken and my commitment to racial harmony questioned, by the grace of God, I stood. My answer to God was and remains a steadfast, "Yes, Lord! I believe it, and I will live it, with Your help and grace."

I came to see that I had put too much stock in people and their perception of me. I had owned the mantle of the "superman" of racial harmony and tried to accommodate every desire as well as deal with every issue that was brought to me. I tried to leap tall buildings of racial exclusion, but I found that the "S" on my chest was only a reminder that I was a sinner who always needed a Savior. I was reminded that unity is God's design, and it has already been accomplished. It was not my job to create it but to maintain it.

While this book was written in 2006, God, in His providence, has delayed its publication until now. Since that time, we have elected our very first African American president for two consecutive terms! There are many people who have declared an end to racism as a result of Obama's presidency. They applaud and celebrate this monumental achievement in America and believe that things are better now. I wonder, however, if the election of Barack Obama was evidence of progress or an exposure of a continual and abiding problem?

Whatever the case, his election has put an otherwise silent issue back on the forefront of the political, social, moral, and spiritual climate of America and the church. In the many places where this material has been presented, some have encouraged me to put these things into print. I was hesitant and put the matter aside until others continually encouraged me to do this.

I present this material with much prayer to the Lord, asking that He would bless it for the use of His church. May the Lord bless us, the church, united by His grace, to be an expression of the glory of God in the world.

CHAPTER ONE

Understanding Our Terms
Finding a Way to Communicate

Defining the Boundaries of Our Language

Healthy relationships involve healthy communication. Ask any couple, happy or otherwise, and they will assign the health or lack of it around the nature of their communication. Healthy communication requires words with meanings that are understood and shared. Relationships involve relating, and relating demands clarity in terminology if the relationship is to be meaningful.

When we consider the challenges that persist when it comes to blacks and whites relating to one another, we see that communication is a major stumbling block. This is not owing to the absence of dialogue since there have been a plethora of talk shows, panel discussions, and television broadcasts seeking to solve the problem. What is lacking is the absence of meaningful dialogue. Communication is not real or authentic simply when people express their feelings but only when such expressions use language that is shared and mutually understood.

Herein lies the focus of this chapter. If we are to see any progress in the church on the race issue, we must give time to ensuring that the language we use is shared and understood by all parties. To achieve the goal of racial unity, churches need to work towards a common language. With this common language, we have the hope of gaining a common understanding of the nature of the problem, agreeing on the path to resolving the problem, and deciding on the way to measure progress or the lack of it.

The history of the church has taught us that terms matter. Christians have died in defense of terminology because of what was at stake in the meaning of the words. It was not enough to state that Jesus was Lord. It mattered what was meant in the use of the terms. I believe that the church today needs to fight with the same resolve for terminology that is Christ-centered in discussing the matter of race in the church. We must not fight in cultural isolation.

Blacks and whites must not be content with those of their cultural persuasion agreeing with them. In many ways, this represents the choir talking to the choir. Instead, the fight must be waged with the goal of shared understanding between cultures so that meaningful movement towards gospel demonstration and expression is evident. This is imperative since the history of America (the present included) proves that when blacks and whites communicate using terms that lack shared meaning, the racial divide increases.

One need look no further for proof of this than in the use of the term "racism." This has been and remains one of the most problematic words in our vocabulary. The tension arises not because the term lacks definition but because we lack a shared understanding of its meaning. The term has been adjusted and changed over time in an effort to justify specific racial and cultural assumptions on all sides. These justifications have created such a variety of meanings that the word has ceased to be useful for meaningful dialogue.

The Ambiguity of the Meaning of Racism

Historically speaking, the term has not always been as problematic as it is today. Webster defined racism as "racialism" or "a doctrine or feeling of racial differences or antagonisms, especially with reference to supposed racial superiority, inferiority or purity; racial prejudice, hatred, or discrimination."[1]

There was a time when the term had widespread acceptance, but in our day it has become ambiguous. So ambiguous is the term that there are some who would say that racism no longer exists while others point to specific realities which they deem to prove otherwise. Note such works as Dinesh D'Souza's *The End of Racism*[2] and Derrick Bell's *Faces at the Bottom of the Well: The Permanence of Racism*.[3] The intelligently articulated but varying views of these two men demonstrate the further divide that is sustained in our country and even in the church because of a failure to get at a commonly understood meaning of racism.

If you asked one hundred people what racism meant, you might get as many differing responses. It is not simply because we see the world differently but because we see the world culturally. Whites would give definitions that place most of the negative emphasis on blacks, and blacks would do the same regarding whites. All would probably express that racism is wrong, even immoral, but they would come short of seeing that their definitions—their understanding of the terms—may well be part of the continual problem.

How we deal with racial issues is reflective of how we understand racism. When blacks play the proverbial race card, this demonstrates that some feel race to be politicized and a means of manipulating for justice purposes. While there is clear evidence where this may be the right assessment because it has been used falsely in so many ways, this category is polarizing, not uniting.

Whites, on the other hand, may conclude that racism is dead or a nonissue because the old, overt expressions, such as segregated schools, neighborhoods, and water fountains, no longer exist. In other words, racism should not be an issue because it is illegal. In this, however, they miss the covert actions that still emerge in a society continually defined by race.

These perspectives rest in the hearts of men and women who comprise the church of Jesus Christ. Within the church, these are hidden, unexpressed assumptions that lie dormant until issues like Michael Brown and the events in Ferguson, Missouri, bring them to the surface.

It is hard to believe the kind of chaos that takes place between men and women who love Jesus when the racial problem takes center stage.

It is not because they feel differently about the problems that come due to racial division but because they don't have a shared way to talk about them. We speak from our culture-driven perspectives framed by our culturally determined terminology, which never translates cross-culturally.

The Problematic Use of "Racism"

These varied understandings pose a difficulty in pinpointing what racism is in principle and make the term problematic in discussions within the church. Each view above seeks to modify the standard definition by adding to or subtracting from it in an attempt to show greater understanding of the issue. This sustained ambiguity led Thomas Sowell to conclude:

> [W]ith varying degrees of explicitness, these tendentious ideological redefinitions of racism have become so intermingled with the straightforward meaning ... that the word may be irretrievably lost as a specific, meaningful concept.[4]

In many ways, I agree with Sowell. Varied and contradictory definitions held out as being equally true may sit well with our postmodern, relativistic way of thinking, but they cannot be embraced as the conclusion of the matter.

If the church is to make progress in this area, we must endeavor to understand what is conceptually meant by "racism" and then work hard, together, to find wording that will foster an atmosphere of healthy communication and community. The goal of our communication must always be edification (see Ephesians 4:29), and the way we talk about this term must move us towards unity for all in the church. Since the term "racism" is loaded with so much history, ambiguity, and potential for division, I am of the impression that it is no longer a helpful term in the pursuit of racial harmony.

How then shall we talk about it?

Towards a Shared Understanding

Instead of "racism," I prefer the term "exclusion" as articulated by D. A. Carson in his book *Love in Hard Places*. There he defines exclusion as "all patterns of exclusion of others grounded in race or ethnicity."[5] Carson derives this terminology and definition from Miroslav Volf,[6] who chooses the word "exclusion" instead of "racism" in an attempt to remove the emotional and psychological barriers associated with its use. I think this term is helpful for three reasons.

First, while "exclusion" is not without its own difficulties and questions, it does not have the cultural history that racism does. Second, it eliminates the false notions that the race issue is the problem of a single culture or simply a white problem. The act of excluding is something that blacks and whites have engaged in and continue to engage in. While, historically speaking, whites maintained this divide, blacks have jumped on board with similar actions and expressions of exclusion. Acknowledging that all play a part is essential to moving forward towards Christ-centered unity.

Third, the term "exclusion" shows that actions which exclude on the basis of race can be done in covert as well as overt ways. The act of excluding others does not have to be obvious but can be expressed in a myriad of subtle ways.

What, then, does exclusion look like? When one acts in a manner that excludes another person, how is such exclusion expressed? Miroslav Volf notes that, among other ways, we can exclude by assimilation, by abandonment, and by domination.[7]

Exclusion by Assimilation

Volf describes exclusion by assimilation in this way:

> You can survive, even thrive among us, if you become like us; you can keep your life if you give up your identity ...; we will refrain from vomiting you out ... if you let us swallow you up.[8]

This kind of exclusion is the most common, and it is also, more than the others, deceptively dangerous. While this kind of exclusion may appear to be accepting of an individual, it is actually a rejection of the individual. As Volf states, this kind of exclusion embraces people only when they deny who they are and become just like us.

This is common in churches because it allows the church to appear accepting. When whites come to black churches, the question is not whether they are welcomed but whether they are welcomed for who they are and all that they bring. Can they remain who they are, or will they have to check their culture at the door? The same could be asked of Anglo churches.

I have witnessed over the years that churches can be very welcoming. Their mission statement can be Christ-centered, and the people that greet everyone at the door can be incredibly friendly. Yet, with all of these things being true and genuine, the church can still be actively excluding many visitors and members by assimilation. This is not intentional, but it takes place because we are not making sure that it does not take place.

I have seen blacks and whites leave churches that were friendly but that excluded at the same time. Whites felt they needed to be black in order to fit, and blacks felt that they needed to become white, culturally speaking, in order to fit in the church. No one said anything negative or did anything that angered them. They simply never felt like they, culturally speaking, counted.

Exclusion by assimilation stands ready, though not in overt ways, to spit out that which is different. Individuals and churches like this stand, albeit quietly, opposed to anything or anyone whose culture would evince a version of Christianity that is different from their own. It acts on the unspoken premise of ethnocentrism, the belief that one's culture is superior to all others.

Churches, therefore, must understand their culture and aggressively work to ensure that others are accepted for who they are and are not excluded by assimilation because of what and who they are not.

Exclusion by Domination

This leads to the second form of exclusion: exclusion by domination. Volf comments,

> ... we are satisfied to assign to 'others' the status of inferior beings. We make sure they cannot live in our neighborhoods, get certain jobs, receive equal pay or honor; they must stay in their proper place, which is to say the place we have assigned for them.... We subjugate them so we can exploit them in order to increase our wealth or simply inflate our egos.[9]

The history of America is a motion picture that has played out this kind of exclusion in many ways. From the disenfranchisement of the Natives to the enslavement of Africans, the settlers were complicit in engineering a psychological otherness that would exist as sure as the new country they would build. This sense of superiority would not cease in the maturity of America but would remain a stain that would almost divide it in the Civil War.

In their book *Divided by Faith: Evangelical Religion and the Problem of Race in America*, Michael Emerson and Christian Smith give illumination to this aspect of exclusion. They write of what they call a racialized society:

... a racialized society is *a society wherein race matters profoundly for differences in life experiences, life opportunities and social relationships.* A racialized society can also be said to be 'a society that allocates differential economic, political, social, and even psychological rewards to groups along racial lines; lines that are socially constructed.[10]

This kind of inequity still remains in our culture and society. Moreover, these inequities are the result of an exclusion that is unspoken and, today, unwritten.

While exclusion by domination can be viewed as a structuring of society on the basis of status and value, it must be considered as something more than this. Exclusion by domination is also mental. It is in the intellectual that we see the perpetuation of the structural. We dominate those to whom we assign a lesser status than ourselves.

Historically speaking, Anglo Christians had to assign to blacks a status that was less than human in order to feel justified in treating them as less than the image of God. In an odd way, they were preserving their faith as they brutally enslaved Africans. Note the progression: they had to intellectualize their evil desires in order to follow through with them. It did not end there, however.

America, as well as the church, was built on such rationalizations. Within evangelicalism lies the unspoken belief of the superiority of the Anglo church and the inferiority of the black church. This edifice has not only been built but also fortified in the psyche of the church and society. Where the fortress is not intentionally destroyed, it is accepted as an appropriate rule of governing.

I think that one of the most important steps that the white church can take is to speak against the unwritten and unspoken perception that white is better and best. It would be healthy for the cause of unity with Christ if we all began to recognize that we live in a culture where we are constantly bombarded with visuals and articles that perpetuate the belief that crime, abortion, poverty, broken families, and unintellectual churches are predominantly in the black community.

Anyone who is mildly aware of economics understands that money follows perceptions. Low perception means low funds, and low funds ensure a lack of success and continuity. We invest in what we trust and believe in, and if a particular community has been assigned low or inferior status, we are reluctant to invest there.

From the perspective of the church, we can now see how this form of exclusion impacts and retards efforts towards racial harmony. Evangelicals usually fail to challenge the system, not just out of concern for evangelism but also because they support the American system and enjoy its fruits. They share the Protestant work ethic, support laissez-faire economics, and sometimes fail to evaluate whether the social system is consistent with their Christianity.[11]

Exclusion by Abandonment

Volf explains exclusion by abandonment in this way:

> Like the priest and the Levite in the story of the good
> Samaritan, we simply cross to the other side and pass by,
> minding our own business (Luke 10:31). If others neither
> have goods we want nor can perform services we need, we
> make sure that they are at a safe distance and close
> ourselves off from them.[12]

This kind of exclusion suggests that while we recognize
the crisis and the pain in the lives of other people—black
or white—we simply turn the other way as if what we
have witnessed is merely an aberration.

This third form of exclusion is becoming increasingly
prevalent not only in the way the rich of the West and
the North relate to the poor of the Third World but also
in the manner in which suburbs relate to inner cities and
the jet-setting "creators of high value" relate to the
rabble beneath them.[13]

I remember watching the movie *Hotel Rwanda*. It
described the horrors of what was nothing short of
genocide in the city of Rwanda in 1994. In the movie,
Paul Rusesabagina is looked to as the one to lead and
seek protection for the Hutus, but he is initially crippled
by his own naiveté. He believes that if the United
Nations knew of what was taking place, they would
surely come to the rescue. One reporter, eager to get
scenes of the horror on tape, goes out into the cities and
captures images of the mass numbers of slaughtered
Hutus.

When he becomes aware that Rusesabagina is
watching the footage of the carnage, the reporter turns to

him and, with a sense of shame, apologizes for showing this footage of dead bodies along the roadside. Rusesabagina turns to him, not angered by the footage but with a sense of excitement. He feels that when the UN sees this, they will *have to* come and help. To this unwarranted glee, the reporter states a chilling reality. He says that when individuals watch the footage, they will simply view it, turn around, and continue eating dinner as if nothing were wrong.

This is descriptive of many Christians and churches in the United States. When we see the horrible realities across the world, we are inclined to turn away and continue in our daily activities, untouched and unaffected. At times it is because we feel powerless to make a difference, but if we are honest, we will admit that we find our affections at odds with the command of Scripture to "weep with those who weep" (Romans 12:15).

How many of us worship in churches located in areas riddled with poverty, hunger, educational deficiencies, and limited job opportunities and look the other way? How many drive into the hood from the suburbs to worship but give little thought to those who surround their place of worship? How many live in areas where churches are suffering financially, neighborhoods are ravished, and children go to bed without food, yet they remain emotionally aloof, unmoved by the suffering around them? In these ways, we exclude by abandonment.

Again, if we are to have intelligent and meaningful conversations about racism, we must come to terms with our terms. Racism is an old, antiquated, and ambiguous term. Exclusion by assimilation, domination, and abandonment are the phrases that I propose we use since they speak to the multifaceted nature of the divisions related to race. There may be others that are useful, but whatever terms we use, we must find agreement in meaning.

Racial Harmony

This leads to another term that we must give attention to: racial harmony. There have been many ways in which this concept has been expressed, but I have found "racial harmony" to be a helpful expression of what we are seeking as a goal in the church.

What we are after is the genuine expression of the unity established by Jesus in and through the cross. Unity is more than a physical expression (diversity). It is primarily about the heart that is prompted by the gospel to love the nations than it is about appearance. Those who love racial harmony are not content with simple diversity but long for this diversity to lead to a kind of union that expresses itself in deep and meaningful relational bonds.

To that end, I propose the following definition of racial harmony as the guiding terminology within the church. Racial harmony is the intermingling of all that is right, true, and biblical within various cultures for the purposes of a fuller expression of the glory of God in the church and in the world. Within this definition, there are several principles that can be lifted to offer further illumination and instruction.

The design of God in redemptive history is the display of His glory in the united diversity of His church.

I will deal with this aspect of the glory of God in more detail later, but a brief word is needed here.

History is not cyclical but linear. God is not moving in circles but is headed towards a definite end, namely the exultation of His glory in all the nations. The resolve for our pursuit of racial harmony is not just harmony for the sake of harmony but harmony for the sake of the glory of God. Everything that God is doing in redemptive history is for His global glory, and racial harmony is His design and a chosen means to display His glory.

Every culture has something to contribute to our understanding of the character of God and His workings in redemptive history.

One of the foundations of racial exclusion is the feeling of ethnic or cultural superiority. Other cultures, it is assumed, lack the ability to add to one's own culture intellectually or spiritually. This kind of thinking undermines a very essential factor that must be embraced if we are to be encouraged to move towards racial harmony.

We must be governed by the truth that other cultures have experienced God and, therefore, have something to contribute regarding the work, ways, and character of God. When God ravishes a soul by grace and calls that person to Him, He has put on the garb of that culture and sanctifies it as an expression of His grace to the world. The overarching point behind this is the fact that the beauty of God is spread out over the diversity of His people. We cannot afford to miss this.

God's beauty is so incomprehensible that it cannot be expressed in one culture. More than this, God is too big to be confined to one culture, and our cultures are too limited to presume that they house the whole of what can be understood about God. The way in which He works in a culture is an expression of Himself in ways that cannot come from another culture.

God speaks not only in the theological writings of Europeans about how and what to believe about Christ; He also speaks through the perseverance of the Africans and slaves in showing how to persevere in Christ. Interestingly, scholarship is beginning to discover something of a theological cover-up regarding the origins of what is deemed Western theology. Thomas C. Oden has written a compelling and documented book titled *How Africa Shaped the Christian Mind: Rediscovering the African Seedbed of Western Christianity*, in which he argues that orthodox theology was both taught and practiced in Africa before it ever appeared in its dominant European context.[14]

From the doctrine of the Person of Christ to the very format of Western theological councils, Oden makes it evident that these Western activities were secondary to their African origins. This proof that Africa played the major role in the doctrinal development of the church demonstrates that Africans were not the recipients of Christianity; rather, they were the originators of its doctrinal formulations.

Again, every culture has something to contribute to our understanding of the character of God and His workings in redemptive history, and to deny this is to limit our understanding and worship of Christ. We must come to see and appreciate God's ways and workings in and through other cultural expressions since God works in a way that is unique to each.

Anything that is considered beneficial from any culture must be considered as such only when it is Christ-centered.

The error of multiculturalism is its undiscerning view of cultures. Its premise is that whatever any culture believes and holds as true must be considered good, acceptable, and useful to the masses even though, for the Christian, it may present ideals that oppose Scripture.

The pursuit of racial harmony and the exhortation to see God at work in other cultures is not the same as sanctifying everything in every culture. There is a point of reference which must center and guide our thinking, talking, and activities towards racial harmony. That reference point is the gospel of Jesus Christ. As an African American, I do not embrace some things within my own community because of my convictions of what the gospel is and what it means as it relates to life and faith.

This is not a denigration of my culture but a gospel-centered assessment of my engagement with it. The call for all of us—black, white, Hispanic, etc.—is not to think culturally but to think, first and foremost, as Christians. Miroslav Volf says it best when he writes:

> Christians can never be first of all Asians or Americans, Croatians, Russians, or Tutsis and then Christians. At the very core of Christian identity lies an all-encompassing change of loyalty, from a given culture with its gods to the God of all cultures. A response to a call from that God entails a rearrangement of a whole network of allegiances.[15]

The call is clear: the gospel must inform my thinking, my relationships, and my assessments of my own culture. My culture must not inflict itself on my Christianity.

It is not helpful or biblical to embrace culture for culture's sake when I say that Jesus is my Lord. If Jesus is my Lord, His Lordship extends to every aspect of my life and claims it for Himself. Racial harmony demands that we keep the gospel central in order to inform and even correct our feelings and actions with respect to our respective cultures. It is and always must be our motto: Christ above culture.

The church is to be a witness and leader in the world on the issue of race relations by demonstrating in her unity the essence of true unity, Jesus Christ.

One thing that the church must understand and embrace is that the world, regardless of the amount of money, energy, and effort it gives to this, cannot express unity in its true essence. This is because the essence of unity is found in a right knowledge of the Person and work of Jesus Christ, whom the world denies.

God has granted the history of the church in the United States a wonderful opportunity to make much of the power of the gospel in demonstrating unity in her own ranks. The church is full of people affected by the evils of exclusion. In fact, there are pastors, deacons, and members whose very existence was once dominated by excluding on the basis of race. There are others who, victims of the evils of exclusion, struggle to feel gospel affections towards whites. They may have been sympathetic to the ideas of the Ku Klux Klan (KKK), or they could have been advocates of the militant black power movement, but by the grace of our Lord, they have been met by the saving power of the gospel.

Both groups now, by the grace of God, stand in a unique and powerful position to show the transformative power that the grace of God can have on a person's life and affections. What a beautiful thing this would be in the world if such men and women of Christ consistently declared and demonstrated their mutual love not only for Christ but also for one another! The world is looking for unity, but only the church can demonstrate what it is and lead the way.

Jesus says that His disciples are to be the salt and light of the world (Matthew 5:13-16). These descriptions are metaphors which include the church's role and goal in racial harmony in the world. As salt, the church is to act in ways that arrest the decay of sin in the world because of exclusion. We are to touch that which is insipid and make it flavorful. In our unity, we show the world what the gospel has accomplished.

As light, we are to shine where the darkness of racial division and exclusion seems to reign. Any exclusion, especially on the basis of race, is a darkness that stands in desperate need of the light of the gospel. The people of this world need us to express the unity that Christ has achieved and accomplished on the cross so that they may be freed from their own sin and rebellion.

The church needs to be on the forefront of the pursuit of unity because true unity can only exist where Christ is central to the heart and affections of each individual. Attempts at unity from the world are only mildly effective since it is unity of the external, not the internal, kind. The world needs to see unity not only achieved but sustained and expressed in the lives of Christians. The only way this can take place is by the sustaining power of the gospel at work in our hearts.

Racial harmony is community specific and heartfelt.

When I say that racial harmony is community specific, I mean that racial harmony is going to look different in different churches based on the look of the community. For instance, imagine a church located in a town where within a ten-mile radius, there is only one predominant culture. What would racial harmony look like in a church in such a setting?

Since such a church could only reflect the dominant culture, how could they be compelled to pursue racial harmony when the surrounding towns are not diverse? Should this particular church be held to the same standard as every other church regarding its reflection of racial harmony within the church? I do not think this is right or fair because it is not likely. Context means something.

A church in Beverly Hills will look different from a church on the south side of Chicago because of the kinds of people nearest to them. Churches located in a community where diversity is rich and visible have a responsibility to reach and be a reflection of the community in its makeup.

Proximity implies accountability. In other words, if poverty is what you see outside of the church doors, then there must be a higher commitment to ministering to the poor. If all around your church are people of different colors and cultures, your church has a responsibility to minister to those peoples for the sake of the glory of God and their salvation.

Along with community specific, racial harmony must be understood as heartfelt. While this aspect of racial harmony is important for every church, it is a higher one for those churches located in communities where one culture is dominant. There are those who would hear that racial harmony is community specific and proceed to act, live, and minister as if they are "off the hook" since there is little to no diversity where they are. This is not the case.

Racial harmony is a location issue, but it is also, and more so, a heart issue. For this reason, whether you are in the midst of diversity or not, this must be your heart's desire. A church whose context does not lend itself to pursuing racial harmony in tangible ways is not off the hook. Such a church needs to be challenged to express its commitment in different ways, focusing on the heartfelt aspect of racial harmony.

While it may be unlikely that diversity would ever dawn near some churches' doors, they must stand ready and willing to embrace it if, by providence, a person of another culture is led to attend the church. A heartfelt commitment to racial harmony would allow the church not to be taken off guard by the visitor but instead to be ready for him or her. Their hearts have been prepared and aligned with the global purpose and design of God for the nations so that when the nations attend, they are joyfully received and embraced.

The pastor must lead the church in this way by preaching about the advancement of the kingdom of God and its inclusion of many cultures, connecting it to the magnification for the glory of God in the world.

Communication Is Crucial

The quest for racial harmony is one that stands dependent on many things which will be expressed in this book. One crucial element is clear communication that comes from a shared understanding of our terms.

CHRIST ABOVE CULTURE · 37

Dr. Al Mawhinney, one of my seminary professors, once made a comment about ministering to Jehovah's Witnesses that I have long remembered. He said that if we were not willing to listen to all of what they had to say before we responded to them, we should not engage them at all. To not listen and simply seek to win the battle, he said, was "a waste of kingdom time." I feel the same about racial harmony.

If we are not willing to do the hard work of seeking to listen to one another in order to understand one another, we are not willing to do what it takes to see racial harmony become a reality in our lives and in our churches.

My hope is that many will, if they are not already doing so, seek to flesh out the contents of this chapter in existing relationships.

Chapter 1 Notes

_____

_____

_____

_____

_____

_____

_____

_____

_____

_____

_____

_____

_____

_____

_____

_____

_____

_____

_____

_____

_____

CHAPTER TWO

The Church's Burden
The Complicity of the Church in Cultural Exclusion

The story is told of a woman who had planted her very first rose bush. Over time she began to see weeds grow around the otherwise beautiful roses. What she did next is what any novice would do: she cut down the weeds.

The problem was solved, and the weeds, she believed, would no longer obscure the beauty of the roses. However, she soon discovered that the weeds had appeared once again. So, with shears in hand, she did as she had done the last time. This process would continue a few more times until she finally sought the advice of another who was more experienced in gardening than she was. What she found was both enlightening and shocking.

She was told that her problem was not the weeds but the roots that gave life to the weeds. Even though they were cut down, they would keep appearing. She discovered that the problem was not what she could see but what she could not see. The same is true when we speak of the racial divide in America and in the church.

If we are to weaken the impact and presence of racial exclusion in the church, it is not the appearances or evidence of it that should occupy our attention and focus. Like the woman above, we must be instructed to go deeper and discover the roots that keep racial divisions alive. What we will learn is that our current struggles in the church are not new and the church has actually done much to preserve this division.

While the issues of division today are present tense, they are the result of historical roots that formed the seed for their existence and continuation. The aim of this chapter is to show that the church's present-day problems of racial exclusion are not actions that come out of a vacuum but, rather, are the result of deeply rooted beliefs about the nature of Africans and the subsequent justifications of the institution of slavery, which the church affirmed.

American Slavery vs. Slavery in the Bible

One of the most-asked questions regarding slavery in America is how it differs from the slavery we read about in the Bible. On one hand, this is not an easy question because the Bible, our guide for faith and practice, highlights and does not bemoan the idea of slavery. It seems to offer workable solutions to societies with hierarchical structures. On the other hand, we find texts in the Bible that forbid a certain kind of slavery, and it is here that we see the distinctions.

Some have attempted to equate the practice of slavery in the Bible with the slavery of America, but the two can never be reconciled. D. A. Carson offers a helpful historical picture:

> In the West, none of the slavery was the result of free people selling themselves into slavery because they were bankrupt. More important, in the Roman world, there were slaves from many different races and cultures: slaves could be British, from the Italian peninsula, Jewish, African and so on. But there were also free individuals from all those heritages and some of these were learned and influential. That meant that there was little identification between slavery and one particular race. By contrast, in the West from the beginning almost all blacks were slaves and certainly only blacks were slaves.[16]

Murray J. Harris, in his book *Slaves of Christ*, offers two prohibitive marks of slavery that distinguish American slavery from that in the Bible: "the exploitation of the slave for monetary gain" and "the kidnapping of persons for slavery and trafficking in slavery."[17] Whatever one will say of slavery in America, it cannot be denied that the prohibitions articulated by Harris were actions that formed the core of the enslavement of Africans in this country. This being the case, we cannot draw a line from the Bible to American slavery without noting such differences.

One cannot deny the deafening silence of Christ on this issue and the ambiguity of Paul, though he gives mention to slavery. Slavery was not condemned in the

New Testament, but it is also without dispute that the slavery of the Bible was markedly different from American slavery.

In the Old Testament, slaves could accumulate property and could, with such accumulated money, buy their own freedom. It does not take much to recognize that promises of forty acres and a mule were never realized. Furthermore, slaves were rigorously protected from inhumane treatment under the Law. If a slave was murdered, the murderer would be killed, master or otherwise (Exodus 21:12). If a master knocked out a slave's tooth, the slave was to be set free (Exodus 21:27). It is clear that no law existed in the United States that gave such safeguards to slaves. The historical record is replete with instances of inhumane treatment of slaves, which was rewarded rather than punished.

Even when we consider the New Testament and read such texts as 1 Corinthians 7:20-22, we must give special care not to read an American conception of slavery into the slavery of the Roman world during Paul's time.

Christians through the years have staunchly argued positions both for and against slavery and sought either to justify or denounce it. In *A Defense of Virginia, and Through Her, of the South, in Recent and Pending Contests Against the Sectional Party* (1867), Robert Dabney argues that the slavery of Bible times was, compared with that of America, "barbarous, cruel and wicked in many of its customary incidents, as established both by usage and law."[18]

Modern-day authors such as Doug Wilson find some commonality with Dabney in this regard, seeking to justify slavery: "We have all heard of the heartlessness—the brutalities, immoralities, and cruelties—that were supposedly inherent and widespread in the system of slavery."[19] Wilson tries to prove that such depictions of slavery were "a great deal of falsehood paraded about in the pretense of truth."[20]

Yet, alongside these voices, I hear other voices stating the opposite with equal vigor. I read John Wesley's letter of encouragement to the embattled but perseverant Wilberforce, saying of American slavery that it was "the vilest that ever saw the sun."[21] I read of Samuel Hopkins declaring "slavery as 'contrary to the whole tenor of divine revelation' and 'a horrid reproach of divine revelation' to suppose that the Bible should be used to support enslavement."[22]

As for Dabney, I will conclude that such a compliance with slavery is owing more to cultural hermeneutics than the Bible. As for Wilson, I will believe the description of John Wesley, who was living during the time of slavery, more than one whose hermeneutic was culturally informed. I suspect this debate will continue until Christ returns since men on both sides express an uncompromising commitment to truth.

Whether consciously or unconsciously, men throughout the history of the church have failed to see the opposition of American slavery to the heart of Christianity expressed by our Lord in these words:

You shall love the Lord your God with all your heart and with all your soul and with all your mind. This is the great

and first commandment. And a second is like it: You shall
love your neighbor as yourself. — Matthew 22:37-39

Essentially, love for God finds an expression in our love for our neighbor(s).

In reading the writings of men whom I would consider theological giants, I have found, with some, that their actions and statements regarding slavery were shockingly inconsistent with biblical Christianity. It is not so much what they have stated as the hypocrisy of their words and life regarding the purpose of Africans.

I have come to understand and embrace the phrase of my seminary professor, who said that all of our heroes have clay feet. They are fallible, sinful human beings who, like all Christians, possess the potential of acting inconsistently with what they believe. Never has this reality been more helpful for me than in considering men's words and writings on this subject.

In showing the church's burden in the present and continual problem of racial exclusion, I will highlight the lives of three men whose writings and ministries gave significant shape to the growth and expansion of Christianity in North America: Jonathan Edwards, George Whitefield, and Robert Dabney. These three are significant, not only because of their standing in Christian history but for other reasons as well.

That Edwards believed and acted as he did on this subject in the North shows that the South should not be seen as the sole perpetuator of slavery and its institution. Whitefield is commonly seen as instrumental to what we know as evangelicalism and is credited with the effects

CHRIST ABOVE CULTURE · 45

of the Great Awakening, yet he affirmed slavery. Dabney is included here because he, being thoroughly orthodox in his theology, represented in his writings the beliefs of the South regarding slavery. These three show us that slavery extended into different time periods (pre- and post-Revolutionary) and different regions (North and South). More importantly, they show how the church played a significant role in sustaining and perpetuating the racial divide.

Jonathan Edwards[23]

Jonathan Edwards is claimed by many to be the greatest American theologian that the church has ever seen. His contribution to the intellectual aspects of the faith as well as the role God assigned to him in revival cannot go without notice or appreciation. Yet Edwards, like all of our heroes of the faith, was a man with clay feet. One area where this is shown is in regard to slavery.

To the day of his death, Edwards was a slave owner. Unlike some in his day, he provided no means for their freedom after his death, thus continuing and affirming the institution of slavery to the end. Edwards's possession of slaves did not come simply through the process of inheritance; he also participated in the purchasing of slaves himself. In 1731 he purchased three: Joseph, Lee, and a woman named Venus. Listed in the inventory of his estate in 1758 was a "negro boy" named Titus.[24]

One irony with Edwards, a staunch believer and defender of orthodoxy, was that he once stood shoulder to shoulder in the defense of slavery with a man whose theological persuasion he vehemently opposed. In this regard, it is right to conclude that his theology took a back seat to his slave-holding priorities.

While it is not known what Edwards knew or understood about the inherent evils of American slavery, it is doubtful that he was totally unaware of some abuses that history records as common within the institution itself. However, whatever knowledge he had was not enough to deter him from participation in it. Apparently Edwards was so at home with the institution of slavery— and the status that it conferred on aristocratic clergy such as himself—that he never really questioned its central tenants.[25] Even so, Edwards is held in high esteem by many who hunger and desire rich, deep, and historically consistent orthodoxy.

This hunger leads Christians to a time in the history of the church when the wells were deep and satisfying, theologically speaking. There is very little dispute that when men and women are reading Edwards, they are reading theology at its best. Yet, this great man, this man to whom many look to find the contours of theological consistency, was a man at home with a system that ripped African men and women from their homeland, tore their families apart, and held them to be inferior beings and second-class humans. They were created by the God of freedom, but because of their skin and the preserved perceptions of their intellectual inferiority, they were treated as something less than human.

This ungodly view and treatment of blacks came not by a man who stood opposed to righteousness and truth, whose mind was stuck in the gutters of unredeemed depravity. This was Edwards, a man whose mind God had touched, who stood in direct contradiction and opposition to truth. This came by the hands of a man considered to be America's greatest Christian theologian! In Edwards, Christianity perpetuated the sin of slavery.

George Whitefield

The influence of Whitefield is without question with regard to the nature, shape, and growth of American evangelicalism. He was called the "'hero-founder' of American evangelicalism"[26] and did more in his itinerant ministry for the advancement of the kingdom of God and orthodoxy than any other of his day. Under his fiery and passionate preaching, the Great Awakening took such shape and hold on America that it stood as a pivotal hinge upon which Christian influence swung. One aspect of its power was seen in the spiritual conversion of both whites and slaves.

Ben Franklin commented on the effect of Whitefield's preaching on those who heard him. Upon perceiving that the offering was about to be collected, Franklin resolved that

> ... [Whitefield] would get nothing from me. I had in my pocket a handful of copper money, three or four silver dollars, and five pistols in gold. As he proceeded I began to soften and concluded to give the coppers. Another stroke of his oratory made me asham'd of that and determin'd me to

give the silver; and he finish'd so admirable that I empty'd my pocket wholly into the collector's dish, gold and all.[27]

Such was the power of Whitefield's preaching. He, too, however, would contribute to the racial divide in America. Whitefield's spiritual influence over many Africans is clear in the annals of history. When he traveled to preach, he would do so to audiences of both blacks and whites. He preached a message, as many did in that day, of radical equality based on the nature of creation and the value of all men made in the image of God.

There was no shortage of spiritual fruit among the African community from Whitefield's ministry. One person of note who shows his impact on Africans was Phillis Wheatley, the first published African American poet. Out of genuine affection for and admiration of Whitefield, Wheatley wrote a poem in his honor at his death.[28]

Another to be affected was John Murrant, who attributes his salvation to Whitefield's preaching. So powerful was Whitefield's impact on Murrant that a brief account of the experience is worth mention:

One day as he squeezed into a crowd attending a revival sermon, Murrant found himself eye to eye with George Whitefield. When Whitefield looked directly at the young black man and proclaimed, "Prepare to meet thy God, O Israel," Murrant collapsed under the force of divine power. As Murrant cried out, Whitefield announced, "Jesus Christ has got thee at last." A new perception of his own depravity and of the devil's presence led Murrant into a mortification so profound that he lay three days without eating....

Murrant recounted, "the Lord was pleased to set my soul at liberty" and "my sorrows were turned into peace and joy and love."[29]

Whitefield's influence on Wheatley and Murrant are but examples of the countless Africans who, Whitefield said, "came to give me thanks for what God had done to their souls."[30] This fact of Whitefield's influence is worthy of note and also telling regarding the purpose of this chapter.

While the aforementioned examples are true, what remains is the reality that while Whitefield preached his message of radical equality in Christ and shared the salvation message with the slaves, he was a supporter of slavery.[31] In this, Whitefield is an example of the kinds of contradictions that we see in present-day evangelicalism—well intentioned but adapting the message to fit the sociocultural, racialized context.[32] He is one of the most interesting cases of evangelical compromise on the issue of slavery.[33]

In the pamphlet *A Letter to the Inhabitants of Maryland, Virginia, North Carolina and South Carolina*, Whitefield stated opposition to what was, to him, a brutish treatment of black men and women created in the image of God. He wrote,

As I lately passed through your provinces, I was touched with a fellow-feeling of the miseries of the poor negroes.... I have no other way to discharge the concern that lies upon my heart, than by sending you this letter. How you will receive it I know not; but whatever be the event, I must inform you in the meekness and gentleness of Christ, that

> God has a quarrel with you for your cruelty to the poor
> Negroes. Whether it be lawful for Christians to buy slaves,
> I shall not take it upon me to determine, but sure I am that
> it is sinful, when bought, to use them worse than brutes.[34]

Whitefield further argued that people of both races are equally guilty with regard to original sin:

> Think you they are any way better by Nature than the poor
> Negroes? No, in no wise. Blacks are just as much, and no
> more, conceived and born in Sin, as White Men are. Both,
> if born and bred up here, I am persuaded, are naturally
> capable of the same Improvement.[35]

It is important to note that what you read in this pamphlet is not a denouncing of the institution of slavery—buying and selling—but a denouncing of the abuses and cruelties of some masters. This ambivalence is the root of Whitefield's contradiction. What he failed to note, consciously or unconsciously, was that the cruel treatment of the slaves could not be separated from the institution of slavery. As long as the institution was untouched, cruelty would always exist, though, admittedly, not among all slave owners. The reasons the Africans were enslaved—being considered less than human—were the reasons they were abused.

When Whitefield ran into difficulties in building an orphanage in Georgia, what once seemed a most vehement attack on the practice of slavery and the underlying principle of Africans' basic inferiority to whites was quickly altered for the sake of pragmatism.

Commenting on this period in Whitefield's life, Dallimore writes,

> Since slavery was not allowed in Georgia they [Habersham and the Bryans] suggested the purchase of a plantation in South Carolina, where, said they, by the use of slave labour, a sufficient income for the Orphan House could be gained ...[36]

Whitefield responded to this proposition,

> God has put it in the hearts of my South Carolina friends to contribute liberally towards purchasing a plantation of slaves in this province; which I purpose to devote to the support of Bethesda.[37]

Dallimore continues with this sober assessment of Whitefield:

> [T]hus, the man of God became the owner of slaves ... in this action Whitefield was making himself a partner in the practice of slavery, with all the inhumanity inherent therein, and while his motive was commendable the means adopted was deplorable.[38]

Whitefield's practice and acceptance of the institution of slavery was one of the faults detected in his life and character and, according to Dallimore, it was grievous and lasted until his death.[39]

Robert Dabney

In the South, there was no one equal in skill, learning, and reasoning to Robert L. Dabney. His understanding and abilities in systematic theology are evident in his book on the subject as well as the overflowing accolades he received from other eminent theologians.

So fierce were his abilities that he was asked, some even go as far as to say he was begged, by Charles Hodge, to teach Systematic Theology at Princeton. As often as he was asked, he declined. Some, like A. A. Hodge, considered him the greatest teacher of theology in the United States. In a lecture on the life of Dabney, Ian Murray spoke of one man who claimed that he was the greatest teacher in the world!

In that same lecture, Murray recounted an incident regarding a man who, having neither seen nor heard Dabney speak, visited a church where he found the pastor absent and a visiting preacher assuming the responsibilities on that particular morning. The preacher began to preach and reason from the Scriptures with such clarity and unction that the man concluded, from this alone, that the preacher must himself be the great Robert Dabney.

Indeed, it was Dabney, and such a remarkable thing as this tells us something of the man's brilliance and influence, which should not be dismissed or forgotten. At the same time, it must not cloud our judgment and heart on the issue of slavery in America. That he is mentioned in this context is owing to the fact that his sentiments regarding slavery are not deduced from brief sentences or thoughts of others concerning him.

Instead, what we know of Dabney's position regarding slavery comes from a book he wrote, seeking to defend the integrity of his native Virginia and the whole South. For Dabney, like other Christians seeking biblical grounds for slavery, the overriding factor was that such an institution was according to nature, being sanctioned by God Himself.

Dabney writes,

> Men ask, "Is not the slavery question dead? Why discuss it any longer?" I reply: Would God it were dead! Would that its mischievous principles were completely a thing of the past as our rights in the Union in this particular are. But in the church, abolitionism lives, and is more rampant and mischievous than ever, as infidelity; for this is its true nature. Therefore the faithful servants of the Lord Jesus Christ dare not cease to oppose and unmask it.[40]

In commenting on this aspect of Dabney's life, David Wells writes,

> Unlike Professor Frank Bell Lewis, who felt that Dabney's major failure ... was his identification with the conservative bibliocentrism of nineteenth-century Virginia rather than with the more liberal Jeffersonian tradition of eighteenth-century Virginia, we would suggest that Dabney was not overly biblical in this subject. On the contrary, he did not go as far as his Bible should have taken him.[41]

It is clear that Dabney understands slavery to be acceptable, and to oppose it is, in his mind, an expression of infidelity. But to whom does he see such infidelity expressed? Not to God, chiefly, but to the South! He goes on to say,

> ... as a son of Virginia, I have naturally taken her, the oldest and greatest of the slaveholding states, as a representative.... In defending her, I have virtually defended the whole South, of which she was the type; for the differences between her slave institutions and theirs were in no respect essential.[42]

A contemporary author and pastor, Doug Wilson, who seeks to have all of us better understand Dabney, admits,

> ... it has to be said that [Dabney's] political views on race-relations hardened after the [Civil] war, and that there was a bitterness here that marred his legacy. That bitterness led him to fight to keep the Presbyterian Church lily-white at the end of the war and the worst thing about this was the fact that Dabney argued from expedience and not from Scripture.[43]

There are other individuals that can be mentioned along with the above that demonstrate the difficulty this issue posed to the church and how some went the way of social, not biblical, conformity. I write about these men not to highlight their deficiencies but to show that the ills of American slavery drew nigh the purity of Christianity and created what Carl Ellis has termed "White Christianity-ism."[44] Ellis defines Christianity-ism as "negative or unchristian religious practices expressed in the language of Christianity."[45]

Edwards, Whitefield, and Dabney each tried to do something positive regarding the issue of slavery but believed and acted in ways contrary to the teachings of the Bible. Their examples prove that the embrace of slavery was a problem not simply for the unspiritual masses of non-Christians but also for men redeemed by the blood of Christ, men perceived and considered the best minds of the faith.

A question that is frequently asked regarding the information above is: How could such men believe and act in ways so inconsistent with the truth they loved? One clear reason is the continuing influence of indwelling sin, which we will address later. Another reason, equally as responsible, is the subtle yet powerful influence of cultural norms and values. What David Wells writes about Dabney could easily be applied to Edwards and Whitefield as well:

> Like all other fallen men, including theologians, he had blind spots where his devotion to the culture made it difficult for him to interpret the will of God.[46]

I raise this point of cultural influence for two reasons. First, it is imperative that we understand these men in their context. To not recognize that these men were products of their time will cause our feelings about them to lack intelligence and be unbiblical. Secondly, the acts of history present an unchanging parable from which we

can understand and engage in the present and
intelligently move forward into the future.

We must consider how their culture affected them so
we may, in turn, be aware of how our present culture
may be influencing the church today. The old axiom is
helpful here: Those who forget the past are bound to
repeat it.

Edwards, Whitefield, and Dabney participated in
slavery and perpetuated the racial divide in America
because they were guided by cultural norms and values
in their interpretation of the biblical teaching on slavery.
Mark Noll, in his book *America's God*, refers to this
interpretive conundrum as "cultural hermeneutics." He
says that the

> ... interpretation of scripture is always caught up within the
> broader interpretation of reality and experience and
> responsibility, in one way or another grounding that larger
> interpretation. What is handed over and appropriated
> always constitutes a vision of meaning," as well as a set of
> specific readings from the Bible.[47]

The cultural context out of which each of these men
lived and ministered was a context in which slavery as
well as the beliefs of inferiority and superiority were
accepted as absolute truths. It was not that only one or a
few denominations condoned the institution of slavery;
all had their fingerprints on the glove of oppression.

Slavery was condoned by all denominations, with the
single exception of the Quakers, and many of the
ministers had slaves to serve them in their homes.[48]

This was not only true in Whitefield's day but was evident from the very start of early colonial history. No truer assessment of what stood before the church regarding her answer to the problem of slavery could be posed than that of the Reverend Albert Barnes:

> The church will affect the institution of slavery, or the institution of slavery will affect the church. It will send out a healthful moral influence to secure its removal, or the system will send out a corrupt influence into the church itself, to mold the opinions of its members, to corrupt their piety, to make them apologists for oppression and wrong, and to secure its sanction in sustaining the system itself.[49]

These were the only options for the church as it grappled with the issues related to slavery. It would act either in cultural compliance or biblical fidelity, but it could not do both.

While slavery was a root in this issue of racial exclusion, there were certain other cultural phenomena that would create higher and stronger barriers against racial unity: the growth of American nationalism and the contributions of philosophical thought.

Before Dabney came on the scene, a certain shift had taken place that would make the battle for freedom and consistent Christianity fierce: the American Revolution. The irony of such a war is that this attempt to be free from the tyranny and oppression of the British was waged by a people who prohibited freedom for others. Freedom, ironically, was being pursued by those who oppressed.

This fact that the oppressor seeks freedom from oppression serves the continuing divide of racial exclusion in America because the oppressor always fears being oppressed. This reality created a barrier of fear between blacks and whites that continues to this day. Whites fear being oppressed (retribution), and blacks fear going back to the days of oppression. This fear has its root in the moral inconsistency of the American Revolution. As great of a war and victory as it was for our freedom, it was fought on morally hypocritical grounds.

Additional information about America's beginning is helpful to understand those days and how they give shape to our present-day tensions. One factor that moved men to revolutionary battle was an intense desire to establish what is known as American nationalism.

This not only gave identity for a new people (the Americans) but also constitutionalized an inferior status of Africans as slaves in America. American nationalism—the expression of American ideals of equality, liberty, and democracy—was formed out of the soil of white supremacy. Though their definitions were extensive in scope, they were limited in their objects. All who were non-European were considered outsiders and unworthy of what these values stood for.

It was not until Lincoln redefined these values in his Gettysburg Address that these terms referred to all people. In his book *The House I Live In*, Robert J. Norrell comments on Lincoln's speech:

[L]iberty, which had originally meant to Americans a freedom from oppressive government, now was expanded to mean also that every person, regardless of race, was free from slavery. Equality, which had originally meant that any citizen regardless of wealth or status was equal to any other citizen in political rights, would come to mean also that people of African descent had the same opportunity for citizenship as those whose ancestors came from Europe. Democracy, which had originally meant that citizens, not monarchs or aristocrats, held the main influence over government would soon be understood to mean that all men, regardless of color, participated in governing the society.[50]

These redefinitions were both short-lived and inconsistently embraced by Lincoln himself.

Lincoln, like a few other Christian abolitionists, understood freedom to mean colonization, not amalgamation. The famed liberator of blacks had no intention of embracing a liberation that would result in *real* equality.

Separation of the races is the perfect preventative of amalgamation," he wrote, and it was both "morally right" and practical for all "to transfer the African to his native clime." Lincoln despised slavery, but when accused of being overly fond of blacks, he said he was not for "social and political equality of the white and the black races," nor had he "ever ... been in favor of making voters or jurors of negroes, nor of qualifying them to hold office, nor to intermarry with white people.[51]

Notable in my reading has been the notion of abolitionism that was inherent in the ministry and writing of Jonathan Edwards, Jr. Remarkably he would come to differ with his father regarding the slavery issue and, along with others, would wage a full assault on those who embraced its evils. Yet, his commitment fell short of full freedom of Africans in America.

> Edwards, Jr., bluntly expressed the unease with which the New Divinity men envisioned a mixed-race society.... Like ... Edwards, Jr., Hopkins was certain that white Americans would be injured by interracial sexual relations that would engender a mixed-race population.... [T]hey also perceived something repugnant in black faces and black bodies, probably, sadly, even in the black men and women who shared their faith.[52]

While such men fought hard and long for the freedom of slaves, they perpetuated, through an inconsistency of their own, the continuing racial divide that is the current problem and frustration in the United States.

This thinking represented the normal philosophical reasoning of the time. There were three major contributors to this racial philosophy: Kant, Hegel, and Hume.

Kant

> The Negroes of Africa have received from nature no intelligence that rises above the foolish. The difference between the two races is thus a substantial one: it appears to be just as great in respect to the faculties of the mind as in color.[53]

Hegel

The Negro race has perfect contempt for humanity. Tyranny is regarded as no wrong and cannibalism is looked upon as quite customary and proper.... The polygamy has frequently for its object the having of many children, to be sold, every one of them, into slavery.... The essence of humanity is freedom.... At this point we leave Africa, not to mention it again. For it is no historical part of the world; it has no movement or development to exhibit.[54]

Hume

I am apt to suspect the Negroes, and in general all other species of men, to be naturally inferior to the whites. There never was any civilized nation of any other complexion than white, nor even any individual eminent in action or speculation. No ingenious manufacturers among them, no arts, no sciences.... Such a uniform and constant difference could not happen, in so many countries and ages, if nature had not made an original distinction betwixt these breeds of men.[55]

In their book *Christianity on Trial: Arguments Against Anti-Religious Bigotry*, Vincent Carroll and David Shiflett wrote,

The antislavery forces thought of themselves as cultural combatants. To their mind, the battle lines were drawn between differing worldviews.... [I]ntellectuals such as Hume "enabled orthodox Christians to make defense of the Africans a defense of religion itself."[56]

John Wesley referred to Hume as "the most insolent despiser of truth and virtue who ever appeared in the world."[57] I can imagine many saying that such philosophers as noted above were not Christians, and thus we should hold their views as the opinions of the unconverted. I would concur, but its suggestion only highlights the present dilemma of our obscure past. Hume, Kant, and Hegel were not Christians, yet before their day, in their day, and after their day, many Christians held the same beliefs regarding blacks and slavery.

The sad reality is that the words spoken by men who were neither lovers of Christ nor lovers of biblical justice are the same as those of men who claimed love for Christ and truth. One man wrote that the generations of the church that follow this generation would

> look back upon the defense of slavery drawn from the Bible, as among the most remarkable instances of mistaken interpretation and unfounded reasoning furnished by the perversities of the human mind.[58]

The purpose of this is not to elevate history to a place that becomes the lens by which we engage and interpret present realities. Rather, it is to briefly show how the church—the keeper and defender of the Word of God—was complicit in the roots of racial exclusion.

This exclusion was a contradiction of our pursuit of freedom. Its presence inflicted harm throughout our history and continues to do so to this day. The church, by embracing and perpetuating the ungodly notions of inferiority and superiority, sustained something that stands in opposition to the cross. Where she could have spoken and made an impact for justice, righteousness, and equality, she rode the wave of culture by speaking and affirming what it affirmed. Volf writes,

> In one sense even more disquieting than the complicity itself is the pattern of behavior in which it is embedded. Our coziness with the surrounding culture has made us so blind to many of its evils that, instead of calling them into question, we offer our own versions of them—in God's name and with a good conscience.[59]

There is a lesson in all of this for us today. We must be careful in our claims that America is a Christian nation since its history was forged in committing a great evil against man and against God's truth. It was *Christianity-ism.* The soil upon which the "great" ideals and values of this country were forged was a soil marred by a sin that gave an ungodly shape, definition, and value to God's created beings of a certain hue.

I am not one to see racial exclusion under every bush, and I do not go looking to find it. Yet, what I have come to know from the record of history, the experiences of older family members, and my own experiences, is that the old assumptions are not dead. In some respects, they continue to hold quite a bit of sway in our present culture and church. I am the first to acknowledge progress, but as Christians, we must live with our eyes open and recognize that what is called progress has not weeded out the presence of racial division, tension, and exclusion.

In *Divided by Faith,* Michael Emerson and Christian Smith call the society we live in a racialized society. It is a society where race matters with regard to employment opportunities, education, and other life experiences. This does not mean closing our eyes to the advances of blacks but, rather, acknowledging, as one slain black leader stated,

> ...if you take the knife out of my back six inches, that's not progress; if you take the knife out of my back that is not progress. Progress is when you heal the wound that the blow inflicted. — **Malcolm X**

There are many who are less than desirous to talk of this aspect of history and more eager to act as if these events had not occurred. They prefer to give exclusive consideration to "historical progress." This is good, right, and helpful, but it is not the whole story. Things are not better because progress is made. Things are not better because certain overt acts of discrimination are outdated. We must consider, as Emerson and Smith contend, that the form of racialization changes:

> If we were designing ways to measure racism in the antebellum era, we might measure racism as the level of agreement with statements like "Darkies are happier being slaves," "Colored people are more like children than adults," "Africans are not fully human," and "It is God's will that Anglos be masters, and Africans be slaves." If we used this unchanging standard, we would find that the

farther removed from 1856, the smaller the percentage of people agreeing with such statements. Again, using present day logic, we would conclude that racism and the race problem were declining, and indeed, say by 1955, we would conclude it had nearly disappeared.[60]

Yet, we know this is not the case.

As a high school teacher of history, I would always press my students to go beyond the mere fact of an event such as the Civil War. I would teach them that as good students of history, they must understand the ideas behind events since when the event itself is over, the ideas of that event continue on. When we understand the ideas behind the actions and activities of the Civil War, we are able to see how the ideas still have strength today. In this way, we are able to perceive the continuing presence of history and its power to influence long after events have passed.

The horrific evils of the Jim Crow and its laws were an extension of the ideology of inferiority. The Civil Rights Movement was a movement of freedom necessitated by the oppression of God-given freedom. The ideologies and motivations that precipitated these events, along with the host of issues that continue to plague our society and churches to this day, prove that we still have much to contend with. History and the brief expression of it in this chapter teach us that we should not sleep on the power of culture.

Today, our churches do not look much different from the churches of ages gone by. There remains a divide deeply rooted in the love of one's culture over and against full devotion to Christ. There remains a love of what it means to be a citizen of our respective culture groups rather than a citizen of the culture of heaven. The church has perpetuated this divide, and we remain complicit. The complicity does not rest on the shoulders of one race or culture but on all colors and cultures who are content with demonstrating a powerless gospel.

Chapter 2 Notes

_____

_____

_____

_____

_____

_____

_____

_____

_____

_____

_____

_____

_____

_____

_____

_____

_____

_____

_____

_____

_____

_____

_____

_____

_____

CHRIST ABOVE CULTURE · 69

Theology and Racial Harmony
How the Knowledge of God Governs Our Pursuit

There are not too many things that can irritate a driver more than a back seat driver giving directions that were not requested. I know this not simply because I have been the recipient of such advice but also because I have given it a time or two to my wife.

What you should know about my wife is that she is not the best when it comes to directions. She can go to a place several times and still not have a good sense of how to get there. I, on the other hand, was born with directional antennas. I try to help her to see that my only aim in giving her directions is to love and lead her like Christ loves and leads the church. I want her to understand that behind all of my directions is my way of saying, "Dear, this is not the best way to get where we are trying to go. I know a *better* way!"

Yet, no matter how much love exudes from the depths of my heart for her good, it never seems to be taken this way. I wonder why? Inevitably in such conversations of love, my wife would say of my suggested directions, "Who's driving the car?"

With one question everything is put into perspective. The driver becomes the leader, and the passenger is the one who simply rides. Here is the point. It does not matter who is in the car so much as it matters who is driving the car. The one driving the car can listen to the suggestions of others and weigh their helpfulness. In the end, however, the real question is, "Who's driving the car?" With respect to racial harmony in the church, we must ask a varied form of the same question: "*What's driving the car?*"

For too long, social and political thought has been driving the way we understand exclusion and the means we use to counter it. Theology has been present, but it has not been dominant. Theology had been relegated to a back seat driver. When she speaks, her ideas are taken as mere suggestions and never as direction. Theology is third to the famed rhetoric of social and political ideologies. Theology has spoken, but it has not won the day, and I believe that this is a major reason why much of the influence of exclusion has had a wedge in the hearts of believers and infected the health of churches. If we are to remove this wedge, we must put theology in its rightful place: the driver's seat.

Understanding the nature of any problem and its solution must begin with an understanding of theology, the study of God. God is the Creator of all things;

therefore, He must be the Original Interpreter of all things.[61] Therefore, in studying theology, we are doing more than reviewing and learning propositions and phrases; we are seeking to know the ways, mind, and judgments of God on the issues in our lives, families, and the world, including racial harmony. As Christians fight and labor for a true expression of racial harmony in the church and society, we must give attention to the ways and designs of God in accomplishing His purposes in the world.

Sociologists and political pundits have made attempts at solving this problem of racial exclusion. The ineffectiveness of many of their attempts is due to their faulty premise and assumption that man, in himself, is able to exert a morality that is both meaningful and lasting. It is the belief that man is the measure of all things and he possesses internal and moral abilities that can bring change in his heart and, thus, on this issue of racial exclusion.

Central to this thinking is a belief that the root of the problem is merely sociological and/or political. The problem with this kind of thinking is that it does not include the mind of God and it avoids the theological aspect of the problem. People who hold to this thinking understand the problem to be one that is exclusively man with man (black versus white) when it is chiefly man's problem with God.

The aim of this chapter is to show that racial exclusion is chiefly a theological problem. It is a division that has roots in man's division with his Maker due to sin and rebellion. This belief presupposes that all relational problems—marital, friendship, racial, etc.—are the result of original sin and that lasting solutions are found only in our understanding of God. We cannot expect to be one with each other if our relationship with God is nonexistent or lacking.

Oneness is more than a mere acceptance and tolerance of one another. It is "complete unity with each other. It's more than a mere mingling of two humans—it's a tender merger of body, soul and spirit."[62] It also implies the methodological means of dealing with the challenges that threaten racial harmony. In effect, theology matters.

The task of theology is the working out of our faith. What we are aiming at in racial harmony is to discover how God calls people of faith to think and act as a family of different cultures in Christ. Therefore, racial harmony is an act of faith that demands a pursuit of the mind and character of God regarding His intended design and purpose of racial harmony. Douglas Sharp, in his book *No Partiality*, shows this connection:

> ... theological thinking is concerned with correlations between the central affirmations of the Christian faith, their biblical-historical bases and their implications for how we regard and conduct ourselves in the world. The primary subject of theology is the identity, character and actions of God; from this comes a secondary subject—our identity, character and actions as those who confess faith in God.[63]

Theology that is truly understood will find expression in the life of the one who professes to know.

When we consider the meaning of theology, we usually think of the common, classical meaning, which is "the study of God." This simple definition comes dangerously close to making theology something of a pursuit of the propositional knowledge of God over the practical expression of that knowledge. For this reason, I have come to appreciate the definition of theology offered by John Frame: "the application of God's Word by persons to all areas of life."[64]

What I love about this definition is that it moves theology from the theoretical to the practical. It shows that theology is not simply a discipline reserved for professional theologians; it is to be considered and practiced in every sphere of a believer's life. Theology, then, is the truth of Christianity in action. This gets at the heart of how pursuing and knowing God impacts our lives, individually and as a church, as it relates to racial harmony.

If evangelism is theology on fire,[65] then it can be appropriately stated that racial harmony is theology genuinely lived out in the community of the saints. To the degree that you understand and cherish a vision of God who is sovereign, gracious, and free in all that He does, to that degree will you love, live, and labor for racial harmony.[66]

If men cherish God, they will love the image of God in all, treating them with respect and dignity, and, more importantly, they will love all who bear the name of Christ. Exclusion is a theological dysfunction that is the result of a culture-centered view of reality. God, speaking through the Apostle John, has a very different perspective. It is one that is driven by the culture of heaven, not the cultures of the earth. John states,

If anyone says, "I love God," and hates his brother, he is a liar; for he who does not love his brother whom he has seen cannot love God whom he has not seen. — *1 John 4:20*

John finds it theologically unthinkable and inconsistent to be a lover of God and hate your brother.

The word 'hate' is a strong word, and there are many for whom this term does not apply, even though they may exclude others. They do so not out of hate but often out of fear and or ignorance. Yet, there is something in the measure of John's words that should prompt consideration on our part: namely, that it is inconsistent to treat a brother as something less than this when we say that we love his Father.

For example, what would you do if friends were in your home, treating your child with contempt? You would probably put them out if they could not change their behavior towards your child. Why is it that we assume God feels differently about the treatment of His kids than we do? Those we exclude in the church are His children, and He has never been pleased with this.

While it is not inconsequential how and what people think of us in this matter of exclusion, God's opinion is of infinite value and worth. Therefore, if we are to be right in our practice and pursuit of racial harmony, we must give concern to the mind of God on the matter. Theology must play a major role in our understanding of the root of the problem and finding a means that is pleasing to God to remedy it. There is more, however, in this connection of theology to racial harmony.

Theology is not only the application of the Word to all of life, but it also refers to another topic: the self-revelation of God in the Bible. The revelation of God in the Bible can be summed up in one word: sovereign. This aspect is not something that we should skip over or think irrelevant to our concern here. When we embrace a vision of God that is sovereign, it guides and instructs us in this pursuit of racial harmony as we consider two specific aspects of His sovereignty: His sovereignty in creation and His sovereignty in salvation.

Sovereign in Salvation

God is the Creator of all men. The *all* includes everyone—red, yellow, black, or white; rich or poor, etc. Since God is the Creator of all men, we share a common origin. When we consider this fact, we see how feelings and beliefs of racial and cultural superiority are a bit delusional. This is Paul's point in Acts 17 as he systematically destroys the false worldviews of the Epicureans and the Stoics:

> *And he made from one man every nation of mankind to live on all the face of the earth, having determined allotted periods and the boundaries of their dwelling place ....* —
> *Acts 17:26*

The Athenians believed themselves to be vastly superior to other cultures because they were given to reason and philosophy. They perceived other cultures to be vastly inferior. Countering this erroneous notion of ethnocentrism, Paul says, in effect, that we are who we are as a result not of culture but of God! The Athenians were not who they were as a result of being better than others or because they worked harder than others. Rather, it was the result of the divine design and plan of God. For this reason, they could not boast in their Athenian-ness.

The implications of this for our day are clear: whites cannot boast in their whiteness as if it were something they created, and blacks cannot boast in their blackness as if it were something they created. As cultures, we are what we are and have what we have by the divine design of God.

There is nothing wrong with embracing who we are and loving the culture in which God has created us. As an African American, I am proud of many aspects of my cultural history, and I am not ashamed of saying that I am proud to be a black man. Others take pride in their cultural history, and such pride should not be ridiculed. To bemoan who we are and to deny the culture to which we belong is to dishonor God, who made it this way. Yet, in all of our love and pride for our histories, we must give great care to separate cultural pride from cultural worship.

The beauty of blackness and whiteness is found in its being rightly related to God. Some years ago, I heard Tony Evans, pastor of Oak Cliff Bible Fellowship, state that "white is only right when it agrees with holy writ and black is only beautiful when it is biblical."

When our cultural pride leads us to behaviors and actions that exclude others, we dishonor the Lord who made us. That God has created all cultures and colors of men makes ethnocentrism not just silly but offensive to God, who created all things beautiful (Acts 10:9-16). This is why it is incorrect to say that we need to be color-blind.

I was speaking to a man one time who said to me, and I believe very sincerely, "Sherard, when I see you, I do not see color. I see Sherard, my brother." From my heart, I believe he was sincere and did not, consciously, mean what that statement implies. To act as if color does not matter is offensive to God, who made color. He did not make men black and then say, "Oops, I meant to make you white." Neither did He make a mistake when He made men white, Asian, Native American, etc.

People make this statement—"I don't see color"—because they want to express their actual aim and desire: to not make color an issue of relationship. However, it is impossible to look beyond what we see. God did not make men black or white for us to say that we do not see what God has made. In some cases, when people make this statement, they are seeking to escape the challenging and transparent process required for harmony. As difficult as the process may be, the means to the end is not denial but embracing the beauty of God displayed in the diversity of culture.

God does not create color for us to look beyond it but, rather, for us to see it and embrace it as God's gift and to give glory to God for the beauty of His creation. Far deeper than the cultural diversity, however, is the unity of mankind, all created in the image of God. To exclude on the basis of culture or color is to offend God because we are rejecting a fellow image-bearer. It is being like God—possessing certain communicable attributes—that unites all of mankind and establishes the basis for mutual respect and care.

This aspect of the image of God moves this issue beyond the church to society. We respect all human beings, regardless of race, creed, etc., not because we find agreement with them but because they are representatives of the image of God.

Sovereign in Calling

All men and women who know the Lord Jesus Christ belong to one another, regardless of their color or culture. This is not simply because they have been created by the same Creator but because they have been *re*-created by God through Jesus Christ (2 Corinthians 5:17).

Salvation is not the result of the works of man. Along with that, salvation is not based on a man's culture or color. Throughout the history of America, there was the belief that peoples of African descent could not be Christians because they lacked the necessary intellectual abilities of reason. There was a time when peoples of color around the world were deemed pagan and animalistic in their worship and culture.

The missionary thrusts of Europeans were based on a desire to *Christianize* such people groups. It is this missionary thrust that gave fuel to the fire of superiority and inferiority with respect to culture. Missionaries went to Africa to tame savage beasts, as it were, and these notions of distinctions do not simply disappear. To be Christian in America meant to be white. Yes, there were conversions of blacks, but the power of influence of Christianity and the way in which it was interpreted and fleshed out in life was by way of majority culture. They were superior.

The God-ordained design of salvation, however, makes any hint of racial and cultural superiority and inferiority anti-Christian. Paul says,

> *Blessed be the God and Father of our Lord Jesus Christ, who has blessed us in Christ with every spiritual blessing in the heavenly places, even as he chose us in him before the foundation of the world, that we should be holy and blameless before him. In love he predestined us for adoption as sons through Jesus Christ, according to the purpose of his will ....* — **Ephesians 1:3-5**

From this passage, we see that salvation is the work of God and began in eternity. The doctrine of election eliminates any grounds of boasting regarding salvation and, therefore, destroys the thinking that other cultures are to be considered inferior. Salvation, which unites us in Christ, is given without respect to person, color, or culture. Paul says that it is the gift of God (Ephesians 2:8-10).

All men are born sinners and unable to seek after God. Every saved sinner must know this in order to be saved. Sin is the great equalizer, shutting the lips of all men of every color and culture who dare to see their culture as superior to others. In this regard, it is quite funny to reflect on how one sinner can think or say that he or she is better than another sinner. We are all from the same root: sin.

This knowledge should lead us to recognize that we, in our wretched vileness, are not different from any other sinner regardless of culture or race. God rescues us from our sin, not because one culture is better than another but because of faith alone, by grace alone. When we recognize that we are saved by grace alone and that there is nothing within us that makes us more worthy of this gift than another, how dare we see another as less than ourselves?

In the book of Acts, we see the priority of racial harmony in the advancement of the church. The call of God to His people was to go to the nations with the saving message of the gospel (Acts 1:8), but the cultural comforts of Jerusalem hindered their efforts. The heart of God for the diversity of the church is demonstrated in the great persecution that occurred in Acts 8. As a result, they scattered, and it is after this that we witness the penetration of the gospel throughout the nations. In Acts, we see the church beginning in Jerusalem but spanning the contours of the known world, ending up in Rome. Many cultures and people were added through this evangelistic thrust.

Acts records another lesson in racial harmony in chapter 10. This is Peter's lesson. The two major characters in this story are Cornelius and Peter. The contrasts between the two are instructive for us regarding racial harmony. Cornelius, the Gentile, is characterized as "a *devout* man who *feared* God with all his household, gave alms generously to the people, and *prayed continually* to God" (Acts 10:2, emphasis added). All of this, and he was without the gospel! Peter, on the other hand, is a different story. Though he was the chief Apostle of Christ, he still battled with issues of racial and cultural superiority.

The next day, as they were on their journey and approaching the city, Peter went up on the housetop about the sixth hour to pray. And he became hungry and wanted something to eat, but while they were preparing it, he fell into a trance and saw the heavens opened and something like a great sheet descending, being let down by its four corners upon the earth. In it were all kinds of animals and reptiles and birds of the air. And there came a voice to him: "Rise, Peter; kill and eat." But Peter said, "By no means, Lord; for I have never eaten anything that is common or unclean." And the voice came to him again a second time, "What God has made clean, do not call common." This happened three times, and the thing was taken up at once to heaven. — Acts 10:9-16

The Lord told Peter that what He has created should never be considered unclean. This speaks not only of animals but of humans as well.

Luke continues the story a bit later:

And while Peter was pondering the vision, the Spirit said to him, "Behold, three men are looking for you. Rise and go down and accompany them without hesitation, for I have sent them." ... So he invited them in to be his guests.

The next day he rose and went away with them, and some of the brothers from Joppa accompanied him. And on the following day they entered Caesarea. Cornelius was expecting them and had called together his relatives and close friends. When Peter entered, Cornelius met him and fell down at his feet and worshiped him. But Peter lifted him up, saying, "Stand up; I too am a man." And as he talked with him, he went in and found many persons gathered. And he said to them, "You yourselves know how unlawful it is for a Jew to associate with or to visit anyone of another nation, but God has shown me that I should not call any person common or unclean. So when I was sent for, I came without objection. I ask then why you sent for me." — Acts 10:19-20, 23-29

While Peter pondered the vision God had given to him, he was instructed to follow three men who were waiting for him.

Peter had no idea where he was going; he simply followed the instruction of the Lord. When he finally met Cornelius, he said something that was powerful given the circumstances: "You yourselves know how unlawful it is for a Jew to associate with or to visit anyone of another nation" (Acts 10:28). This statement speaks to the challenge of the believer regarding racial harmony.

It was not lawful, but God had orchestrated this entire meeting! God's call for racial harmony trumps that which is deemed lawful. By lawful I mean that which is deemed appropriate by our culture. God and the gospel must trump cultural norms.

Now consider this fact: Peter was pondering what exactly the vision meant (Acts 10:17), but after he met Cornelius, he got it! He said, "God has shown me that I should not call any person common or unclean" (Acts 10:28).

As Cornelius further explained what God had communicated to him while he was praying (Acts 10:30-33), yet another layer of ethnocentrism fell away from Peter's heart.

> So Peter opened his mouth and said: "Truly I understand that God shows no partiality, but in every nation anyone who fears him and does what is right is acceptable to him."
> — *Acts 10:34–35*

Peter moved from calling what God has made "unclean" to having the eyes of his heart opened to the mission of God, which has no room for partiality. What are the requirements of belonging to the household of faith? Culture? No. Color? No. Neither of these is mentioned in Peter's revelation. Fear of God and doing what is right are the two qualifications. Theologically speaking, faith and obedience are the twin acts that make men acceptable to God. If God shows no partiality, how is it that His church, His representative on earth, does otherwise? To do so is to behave without fear of God and to lack obedience to Him.

Let's look now at the events in Acts 15. In this chapter, the church is confronted with how to deal with the inclusion of Gentiles. The leaders gathered, and here is the account:

> The apostles and the elders were gathered together to consider this matter. And after there had been much debate, Peter stood up and said to them, "Brothers, you know that in the early days God made a choice among you, that by my mouth the Gentiles should hear the word of the

gospel and believe. And God, who knows the heart, bore witness to them, by giving them the Holy Spirit just as he did to us, and he made no distinction between us and them, having cleansed their hearts by faith. Now, therefore, why are you putting God to the test by placing a yoke on the neck of the disciples that neither our fathers nor we have been able to bear? But we believe that we will be saved through the grace of the Lord Jesus, just as they will." —
Acts 15:6–11

It is not the conclusion that I want you to see but, rather, the thinking and reasoning of Peter. He said that "the Gentiles *should hear the word of the gospel and believe*" (Acts 15:7, emphasis added) and that "God, *who knows the heart ... made no distinction between us and them*" (Acts 15:8-9, emphasis added). This is the great theological truth of this passage. If God, who knows the hearts of men, made no distinction between the Jews and the Gentiles in salvation, who are we to find and draw lines of distinction on the basis of color? Theologically speaking, we are equipped to fight against our tendencies to exclusion by realizing that God makes no distinctions.

It matters not what the color or culture is. God knows the hearts of all men and does not discriminate. That He knows the hearts of men is crucial. It shows that God knows the deep things of man—Jew and Gentile—and still makes no distinction. There, in the heart, Jew and Gentile are alike, and what we can glean from Peter here is that God looks where we are all the same: sinners. He gives no thought or priority to our external appearance. Exclusion occurs when we give priority to the external, to appearance and culture. To deny or exclude another on the basis of anything other than his or her allegiance to Christ, however, is to oppose all that God and the gospel are about.

The gospel speaks about our inner problems, our sin, and provides the remedy first to the soul, which then is expressed in our actions. The whole of the gospel's power is directed inward, but we tend to demonstrate the gospel in the opposite way. We look outwardly, rejecting anything and anyone that is different from us. When we do this, we forget our own condition and, therefore, deal with others while blind to our own sins.

Theology is central to racial harmony because God is central to racial harmony. As we grow deeper in our understanding of who God is and what He desires in the church, we will begin to see that diversity in churches is not bad but heavenly.

We cannot minimize theology or allow any other discipline to hold sway in our discussions and pursuits of racial harmony. It is time for the church to live out the theology of God, the Bible, and demonstrate that genuine, lasting, and infectious harmony can only take place when the love, adoration, and glory of God are the beginnings and the goals.

Chapter 3 Notes

CHAPTER FOUR

The Glory of God

*How the Glory of God Is the Manifestation
and Mission of Racial Harmony*

The Westminster Confession of Faith begins by asking, "What is the chief end of man?" The answer given is that "the chief end of man is to glorify God and enjoy Him forever."

This answer sums up the very reason and design for God's creation of man: that He might receive glory. This is His mission in the world. Greater even than God's design for salvation is His receiving glory from the whole of creation, especially those created in His image. God's saving designs are penultimate, not ultimate. Redemption, salvation, and restoration are not God's ultimate goal. These He performs for the sake of something greater: namely, the enjoyment He has in glorifying Himself. The bedrock foundation of Christian Hedonism is not God's allegiance to us but to Himself.[67]

The Glory of God: God's Mission in the World

The call to racial harmony is the privileged position of being called by God to get on board with His global purposes. It is also the call to participate in the design of redemption, which will end in His being made much of among the nations of the world. This is the heart of the redemptive historical plan of God, and it is this which forms the background to the Great Commission (Matthew 28:18-20).

It is a privilege to be called by God to pursue racial harmony through discipling the nations because harmony in Christ among the nations is a central implication of what God accomplishes in salvation. The following aspects of redemptive history will make this point evident.

The Call of Abraham

In chapter 12 of Genesis, we read of the call of God to Abram:

> *Now the LORD said to Abram, "Go from your country and your kindred and your father's house to the land that I will show you. And I will make of you a great nation, and I will bless you and make your name great, so that you will be a blessing." — **Genesis 12:1-2***

This text, in missional terms, defines the object of God's plans of redemption: the salvation of the nations. God called Abram to leave Ur and go to a place of which he knew nothing, that he might be God's agent of blessing to the nations. In this call of Abram, we see that it has been God's design and purpose from the beginning to gather not simply Jewish people but the nations for His possession. It is as if the eyes of God, while looking on Abram, gazed beyond him to the nations. Abram was chosen to be a blessing to the nations so that God would be glorified among the nations.

Isaiah writes,

> *I will say to the north, Give up, and to the south, Do not withhold; bring my sons from afar and my daughters from the end of the earth, everyone who is called by my name, whom I created for my glory, whom I formed and made. —*
> ***Isaiah 43:6-7***

The beauty of the mission of God is that it is not confined simply to the Old Testament or to Abram but finds its progressive and redemptive fulfillment in the Person and work of the Lord Jesus Christ.

In the gospel of Matthew, we see Matthew's preoccupation with the theme of fulfillment. His gospel, several times throughout, says that a certain event took place or happened "that it might be fulfilled" or something similar to this (see Matthew 1:22; 2:15, 17, 23; 3:15; 4:14; 5:16; 8:17; 12:17; 13:14, 34; 21:4; 26:54, 56; 27:9). Matthew begins his gospel by calling attention to Christ as the Son of Abraham. In the context of the message of the New Testament and specifically in the context of Matthew, this is not something that should be quickly glossed over.

As the Son of Abraham, Jesus is the embodiment of the promise made to Abraham in Genesis 12. It is Christ, the True Israel, in and through whom the promised fulfillment of Genesis 12 comes into reality. Jesus is both the embodiment and the fulfillment of the promise. In Him, all the nations of the world can be blessed by being reconciled to God by faith in Christ alone.

This is how Paul understands Christ's person and work within the history of redemption:

> Christ redeemed us from the curse of the law by becoming a curse for us—for it is written, "Cursed is everyone who is hanged on a tree"—so that in Christ Jesus the blessing of Abraham might come to the Gentiles, so that we might receive the promised Spirit through faith.... Now the promises were made to Abraham and to his offspring. It does not say, "And to offsprings," referring to many, but referring to one, "And to your offspring," who is Christ. — **Galatians 3:13-16**

So it is that the God who calls Abram to leave his home to be a blessing to the nations also sends Christ into the world to be the embodiment and fulfillment of the promised blessing of Genesis 12.

The Commissioning of the Church

In Matthew 28:19-20, we find Jesus, the Son of Abraham, commissioning the disciples (and us) to go to the nations. The Lord of the universe commissions us to participate in the redemption of the nations for His glory, assigning us the privileged position of being disciple makers of the nations. The question may remain as to how this call to go to the nations relates to our pursuit of racial harmony. There are two implications that can be derived from what has been said.

God Opposes Ethnocentrism

The call of God to be His emissaries and agents of redemption in the world is a call that stands in complete opposition to ethnocentrism, the belief or feeling that one's own culture is superior to others. This feeling or belief is at odds with the global purposes of God and His calling on the church.

When Jesus commissions the disciples, He does not call them to make disciples of Jews only—people who look like them and are like them, culturally speaking—but of the nations! He calls them to be family with people who are culturally different from who and what they are. This is the mission that Christ gives to the church, and it is not an ethnic-specific mission.

We see this reality further expressed when we look in the first chapter of the book of Acts. There we hear the disciples asking of Christ, "Lord, will you at this time restore the kingdom to Israel?" (Acts 1:6). Even after the call and commission to make disciples of the nations, the disciples were still very narrow-minded and ethnocentric regarding the kingdom of God. To this question and mindset, Jesus responded,

It is not for you to know times or seasons that the Father has fixed by his own authority. But you will receive power when the Holy Spirit has come upon you, and you will be my witnesses in Jerusalem and in all Judea and Samaria, and to the end of the earth. — *Acts 1:7-8*

In effect, Jesus did two things in this response: He told them that the time of the restoration was none of their business, and at the same time, He corrected their narrow-minded, ethnocentric thinking. They would indeed be witnesses to Jerusalem, a place of comfort, but they needed to get their minds enlarged and realize that God is not a King of the Jews only but of all the nations.

God is not coming for a single nation; He is coming for the church, which comprises "every tribe and language and people and nation" (Revelation 5:9). This is, from beginning to end, the divine drama of God among humanity. Since the call of God is at odds with ethnocentrism, we must have our minds and hearts enlarged to see and embrace the reality that God's plan is bigger than the white church and the black church and every other culturally specific church. God is coming for a church where black, white, Hispanic, Asian, African, and every other nation is counted and valued. Therefore, the gospel will be preached to all nations.

The mission of our God is a mission for His glory among the nations, and God, in great mercy and consumed with His glory, commissions us to be involved in this drama of redemption. It is impossible to fulfill this command if there is ethnocentric reasoning in our hearts and ethnocentric practices in our churches. *You cannot minister to those of whom you think less.*

God Is at Odds with Place

Not only is the call of God at odds with ethnocentrism, but we also find that it is at odds with place.

When God called Abram to go to the nations so that they might be blessed (Genesis 12:1-3), this calling made his departure from Ur not an option but a necessity. While we read of Abram's leaving and marvel at the great faith that Abram must have had in order to do so, we can often miss the emotional element of the decision to leave.

Abram was not called to leave a place he did not like or love. He was not called to leave the ghetto to go to Beverly Hills or to some other place that was inviting. He was called by God to leave family, friends, and, possibly hardest of all, a place of comfort. Ur was all he had ever known. On top of the emotive elements of the call was the fact that he had no idea where he was to go! This would surely make the move all the more difficult.

All of these things being true, he had to move and obey the call since there were implications that extended beyond himself. Miroslav Volf, reflecting on the call of Abram, writes,

> If he is to be a blessing he cannot stay; he must depart, cutting the ties that so profoundly defined him. The only guarantee that the venture will not make him wither away

like an uprooted plant was the Word of God, the naked
promise of the divine 'I' ... inserted ... into his life so
relentlessly and uncomfortably.[68]

If Abram was to fulfill the call of God and be a blessing
to the nations, he had to leave his culture.

To be what God had called him to be, he could not
stay home. He could not remain in the place of cultural
comfort, the place where everything made sense and
relationships were not challenged by cultural difficulties.
He had to leave. Lest we see this leaving as something
restricted to Abram and the Old Testament, consider this:
what we see in the leaving of home by Abram, the father
of the faith, we see also in Jesus, the Author and Finisher
of faith.

Jesus is the Son of Abraham, and if He was to be the
fulfillment and embodiment of the promise to Abram
and bring the light of salvation to the nations, He had to
leave His home in heaven. Christ, who shared glory with
the Father (John 17:5), left this place of comfort and
entered into the discomfort of humanity as well as the
hardships and difficulties of our sin (Philippians 2:5-8),
that we, the nations, might experience and receive the
blessings of God.

The incarnation is the grand model of what it means
to leave for the purposes of blessing. Christ left heaven
and came down to live and dwell as man with men in
order that we might be reconciled with God. Many
among the nations praise God today because of this
divine disclosure and condescension of the Holy to the
vile. To be a blessing, Christ had to leave heaven, and

the wonder of it all is that He did so willingly! His life is our example that the call of God is at odds with place. The same is true for Christians today.

If we are to be a blessing to the nations and fulfill the call of our Christ to make disciples of all nations, we cannot stay where we are if staying denies its fulfillment. We cannot stay in our culture and fulfill the command of the Lord and bless the nations. We must leave in order to bless. For some, the call to leave has meant or may mean leaving the culture of America and going to lay down their lives for the glory of God in another country.

For most, however, it means living out the call at home, and in His providence, God has brought the nations to us in such a remarkable fashion that leaving can mean building a relationship with our neighbors or coworkers. Whatever may be God's plan for us, the reality is this: the call of God is at odds with place, which means being at odds with cultural comfort.

There is something equally powerful that needs to be considered in this call of God. Abram could not be a blessing and stay. Christ could not remain in heaven and be a blessing to humanity. We cannot stay in our place and be a blessing to the nations. In this reality, we see something of the radical nature of the call. Christianity is so radically at odds with place (cultural comfort) that it demands that all who know and love Christ have a change in our allegiances.

Culturally speaking, we are no longer to see ourselves as black Christians, white Christians, Hispanic Christians, Asian Christians, and so forth. When we experience conversion, not only is the curse of sin reversed but so, too, is our self-description. I am not a black Christian; rather, I am a Christian who is black. This is more than a mere changing of the order of words; it is an expression of a Christian view of life and the world.

As a believer, my black culture does not (or should not) define my Christianity. Rather, my Christianity must inform and guide how I understand my culture and teach me what I should embrace and reject within it. The same is true for any Christian in any culture. Volf puts it this way:

> Christians can never be first of all Asians or Americans ... and then Christians. At the very core of Christian identity lies an all-encompassing change of loyalty, from a given culture with its gods to the God of all cultures. A response to a call from that God entails a rearrangement of a whole network of allegiances.... Since Abraham is our ancestor our faith is at odds with place ....[69]

The call of God is a call to the nations, and this call to the nations demands that we be world-Christians. It demands that our culture be the culture of heaven. It demands that we remove ourselves from our culture, not simply to be blessings to other cultures but so that we might biblically understand and rightly interpret our own culture.

At the heart of this continuing racial conflict in the church are the undiscerned desires to remain and not the rightly discerned and obeyed gospel imperatives to depart. We cannot be the blessing unless and until we become comfortable with the challenging command of

God to leave our culture that we might honor His. If we fail to leave and fail to give heed to the heart of the gospel, I fear that we betray the true nature of our heart for Christ and His kingdom. Christianity is at odds with place.

The Glory of God: God's Manifestation in the World

The glory of God has always had a physical representation in the world. When God led the children of Israel by night, He did so with fire. By day, He led them with the cloud. Both are representations of His presence among His children. His glory was also revealed in the Ark of the Covenant. This is clearly seen in 1 Samuel 4. When it came to be known that the Philistines had removed the ark of God, Phinehas's wife named the child she bore "Ichabod, saying, 'The glory has departed from Israel!' … And she said, 'The glory has departed from Israel, for the ark of God has been captured'" (1 Samuel 4:21-22).

Another expression of the glory of God among His people is found in the temple and the tabernacle. These were expressions of God's glory in that they represented the place where the Lord would meet with His people. They were types, of course, since the God of the universe cannot be confined to temples made by the hands of men (Acts 17:24). Both are considered to be possessions of God, being referred to as the temple *of the Lord* and the tabernacle *of the Lord*. They belong to Him in as much as He was their cause for construction and they were the places where His people regulated their meeting with Him.

In the New Testament, we find that the glory of God finds its most significant expression in the Person of Jesus Christ. His miracles declared and displayed the glory of God, with men and women standing in amazement and glorifying God as they occurred. A text that clearly shows this reality is found in the prologue of John's Gospel (John 1:1-18). What makes this reference significant is the context in which it is found. In this text, John shows the connection of Jesus to the manifestations of the glory of God in the Old Testament and lifts them to higher heights by showing that Christ is the personal representation of God in flesh (John 1:1, 14).

Jesus is also compared to the Ark of the Covenant in that He is the Word that was in the beginning. The Ark of the Covenant was the keeping place of the Commandments of God given to Moses. Now Christ, in Himself, is the Word of the Living God, the *logos* (John 1:1). Christ is also the fulfillment of the tabernacle. In verse 14, it says that He "dwelt among us," which is literally translated to mean that Jesus "tabernacled among us." This gives a clear reference to the tabernacle of the Old Testament.

In His Person, Christ is God with us. The tabernacle and the temple were the presence of God among the children of Israel, and now Christ is the tabernacling presence of God in the world. In this light, John says of Christ, "we have seen his glory, glory as of the only Son from the Father, full of grace and truth" (John 1:14). The glory of the Son is the revealed and expressed glory of the unseen God (John 1:18). This is why the Apostle Paul could make an equally glorious statement:

> *For God, who said, "Let light shine out of darkness," has shone in our hearts to give the light of the knowledge of the glory of God in the face of Jesus Christ.* — **2 Corinthians 4:6**

How is the face of Jesus seen today? One way is through the preaching and hearing of the Word of God as it paints a picture of Jesus. Another way men see the face of Jesus is through the portrayal of Jesus in the life of the church. This has significance to the pursuit of racial harmony in that now, in the words of Paul, the glory of God rests in the church:

> *To me, though I am the very least of all the saints, this grace was given, to preach to the Gentiles the unsearchable riches of Christ, and to bring to light for everyone what is the plan of the mystery hidden for ages in God who created all things, so that through the church the manifold wisdom of God might now be made known to the rulers and authorities in the heavenly places.* — **Ephesians 3:8-10**

The church of Jesus Christ is the mystery of God—the mystery being how God would take two groups of people (Jews and Gentiles) who were diametrically opposed to one another and bring them together in real unity, making them one new man in Jesus Christ.

This oneness of the church is for the purpose of her being a demonstration of the "manifold wisdom of God

... to the rulers and authorities in the heavenly places" (Ephesians 3:10). In other words, far from being a second chance or plan B of God for redeeming sinners, the church was the eternal design of God (Ephesians 3:11). It would be through the church that His wisdom would be made known, not simply to man but to the very principalities and powers!

Paul calls this wisdom of God "manifold" (Ephesians 3:10). This word is properly translated as 'multi-varied' or 'multicolored.' In both uses, the term shows that the expression and knowledge of God does not rest exclusively in the Jews but extends to the Gentiles as well. With this manifold wisdom also comes the cultural reality of racial or cultural harmony.

When God made these two cultures one in Christ, the term 'multicolored' gives proof that the church, now Jew and Gentile, had become a demonstration of this multicolored wisdom of God. The phrase "manifold wisdom," according to Peter O'Brien, was

> poetic in origin, referring to the intricately embroidered pattern of "many coloured cloaks" or manifold hues of "a garland of flowers" ... in richly diverse ways of working which led to a multi-racial, multi-cultural community being united as fellow believers in the body of Christ. [70]

Again, the glory of God has always had a physical representation: the Ark of the Covenant, the temple, the tabernacle, and Jesus Christ. Now, in these words of Paul, we find that the church of Jesus Christ is the physical representation of the glory of God on the earth.

This is why Paul proclaims, "to him be glory in the church ..." (Ephesians 3:21). What kind of church? A multicolored church!

The significance and priority of racial harmony is found in the fact that God has ordained that His glory be made known to the world and to the principalities and powers through the multicultural and multiracial makeup of the church. Certainly what Paul has in mind when he speaks of the church here is the universal church. Some will argue that this fact of Paul's universal intentions undermines the use of this text for the local church. However, what is true about the universal church stands as a model for what every local church must seek to imitate.

If this is God's design for the global church, how much more should it be the desire of the local church, which is a micro-reflection of the universal church? Therefore, every individual and every local church must see this teaching in Ephesians as a goal to be pursued. The degree to which we pursue this reality in the church is the degree to which we will see and taste the glory of God and also the degree to which cultures around us will see the glory of God.

Herein is the weightiness of racial harmony: the glory of God is attached to it. It is unbiblical to have racial harmony as something that is so disconnected to the vision of the church that it does not demand anything of us yet speak of it so as not to be accused of its absence. It must have a central place because of its connection to the glory and honor of God. John Piper, speaking at Moody Bible Institute, put it this way:

Part of the problem is that many evangelical believers do not think this issue is a big issue when in reality it is an all-consuming issue because it is critical to the heart of God.[71]

It is, indeed, critical to the heart of God because the glory of God is tied to this diverse and harmonious expression of the multicolored church in the world. People will know that God is real when they see the power of the gospel on display in the unity and harmony of Christians. Jesus, in His High Priestly prayer for Christians, prays,

I do not ask for these only, but also for those who will believe in me through their word, that they may all be one, just as you, Father, are in me, and I in you, that they also may be in us, so that the world may believe that you have sent me. — **John 17:20–21**

What is at stake in our unity is not our personal comfort or discomfort. These are too shallow to hold sway and power in our hearts and affections. What is at stake is the glory and the knowledge of God being poured out and revealed among the nations of Jesus in the world. In other words, theology matters.

Many will agree that racial harmony is a right pursuit, and the historical and present realities in America will make even the non-Christian say that we must learn to live together. Yet, it is not sensibility or mere practicality that will sustain this pursuit until we have achieved a measure of this reality. Our own wisdom and strength are not enough. We must come to see, as Peter came to see, that the God of the universe is a God who shows no partiality.

We must recognize that the knowledge of God matters and that understanding His mind and purposes in the world and through the church are essential to achieving His call and command. May we love the glory of our God and aim for its display in our hearts and churches.

Chapter 4 Notes

_____

_____

_____

_____

_____

_____

_____

_____

_____

_____

_____

_____

_____

_____

_____

_____

_____

_____

_____

_____

_____

_____

_____

_____

_____

CHAPTER FIVE

Racial Harmony and the Cross
Living in the Achievement of the Cross

At the center of the solution to the burdens of exclusion within the church stands the cross of the Lord Jesus Christ. What He achieved there was indeed that which we seek to exhibit and maintain as a healthy visible representation of His grace and glory in the world.

Whenever the issue of racial disunity is broached within the church, the common response regarding its demise is something to this effect: "People simply need the Lord," or "We need to focus on the cross and realize that He has conquered all sin!"

These statements are true; however, those who say such things tend to minimize racial tensions and operate on what Emerson and Smith refer to as the "miracle motif." This is the theologically rooted idea that as more individuals become Christians, social and personal problems will be solved automatically.[72] This is the

106 · SHERARD BURNS

thinking of well-intentioned evangelical Christians around the United States, both black and white.

They believe that if unbelievers would simply embrace Jesus, they would mysteriously stop excluding people on the basis of race and culture. For those who are already Christians, the call is similar. It is believed that if we would simply "keep our eyes on the cross," this bad thing of racial exclusion would be done away with. While I would never, intentionally, deny the power of the cross to change the affections of a man or woman, I do desire for the church to avoid an idolatrous belief in the cross.

This idolatry is rooted in the belief that the cross, as an object, is the cure-all for racial and cultural exclusion and division in the church. This, however, is simply not the case. In fact, the miracle motif actually ends up fostering hearts that exclude. Belief in it allows men and women to think that they are free from acting or behaving in ways that exclude on the basis of race. For them, the mere affirmation of believing in Jesus and what He did on the cross becomes a shield, a deflector, of any accusation of exclusion. In turn, others perceive them the same way, concluding, "He could not have been that way! He loves Jesus!" But unexamined hearts are dangerous hearts.

The history of the Christian church proves this. As we have already seen, history demonstrates that men and women could be lovers of the cross and, at the same time, enslave or affirm the enslavement of Africans. These lovers of the cross could also justify their actions on the basis of a culturally interpreted gospel. This is the church's burden. If this kind of hypocrisy could exist in the lives of saints we respect and esteem, we must come to realize that something greater than a verbal loving of the cross is necessary.

I must quickly admit that I am not seeking to add to the cross, and in no way am I suggesting any insufficiency with regard to it. I am saying that believing in this idea of the cross—the miracle motif—can bring one dangerously close to exalting the thing, the cross, over what Christ actually achieved for us because of it. Far from denying the power and centrality of the cross, I am seeking for a consistency of Christianity in light of the cross.

Since, as believers in Christ, we have the cross standing at the center of our view of life and the world, it is the fleshing out if its implications in our lives that is needed. If the church is to see and demonstrate genuine unity, our commitment to living cross-centered lives must go beyond mere words and rhetoric. It must be expressed in lives that are lived according to the principles of the Bible and the example of Christ.

My heart and desire is that the church of Christ be made up of believers who are not simply concerned with getting our theology right—though we should desire this—but who also desire to reflect right theology in our relationships with one another, across racial lines.

The Place of the Cross in the Pluralism of America

We must ever be looking to the cross and its implications and away from the world, which, at every front, attacks the very heart of our hope. This world is not a friend of grace to help us to God. In fact, the greatest threat to any type of unity in the church is not the call to deny Christ but, rather, to dethrone Him.

In our day of postmodern relativism, we are no longer hearing the out-front reasoning of old that simply denied every aspect of the fundamentals of the faith, such as "Christ is not God," "Christ is not the Savior of men," or "There is no such thing as the supernatural." These claims still exist, but what we are seeing today is a system of belief that says everyone can be right regardless of whether or not one person's beliefs contradict everyone else's.

At the core of this thinking is the idea that the only absolute truth is that there is no absolute truth. This claim denies the absolute truth and trustworthiness of the Bible. Such claims of truth are divisive. The great theological truth of our day, so says the world, is that everyone is right except those who deny that everyone can be right. If there are any who believe in a truth that is universal, such as the exclusivity of Christ, they are opposing the great ideals of humanity and spirituality, not to mention tolerance. Christians cannot shy away from these philosophical ideas because they have more influence over our culture and even some of our thinking than we might suppose. Understanding this is crucial to our fight for racial unity in our lives and churches.

Historically, the United States has been referred to as the great melting pot. People from around the world have come, filled with hope for a greater freedom, with aspirations of pursuing and attaining the American dream. This has been deemed one of the great features of our country. Many can come and, if they work hard, make a living and provide for their families here and in their native country. However, with the realities of such freedom has come a confusing and blurring of the lines as it relates to the idea of universal truth and equity. The idea of a melting pot has given way to what is known today as multiculturalism.

Multiculturalism

Multiculturalism is the outgrowth of postmodern relativism, which holds that truth is a socially constructed reality that is determined within specific communities or culture groups. What one group calls true is not binding for all groups since every group has the authority to determine its own truth. Multiculturalism maintains that everything about every culture in America must be deemed legitimate if we are to be a free society and truly American. Any claims of universal truth are quickly dismissed as un-American and insensitive. Within this ideological framework, the meaning of unity, religiously speaking, has been changed from agreement around certain truths and principles to the acceptance of ideological diversity.

At the core of this reasoning is the idea that unity is not the result of agreed-upon beliefs but, rather, tolerance. However, the veneration of tolerance peddled by postmodernists is actually a twisted and dangerous corruption of true virtue.[73] They claim that it is the highest act of respect to be tolerant of what others believe even though we may consider their beliefs to be contradictory and detrimental to the God of truth. Christians, they say, are intolerant and narrow-minded because of our exclusive claims concerning Christ and truth.

What is interesting at this point is that postmodernists betray their own system of tolerance. They do not show tolerance to the Christians' belief in the exclusive claim of Christ as Lord and the Bible as absolute truth. Diversity, in this way of thinking, is a mindless diversity. It is a wholesale acceptance of everything within every culture, and they do this as a means of diversity and equality.

Homosexuality is defended on the basis of relative truth. The culture says, "If it works for them, who are we to say they are wrong?" Diversity training in companies is often, though not overtly expressed in this way, geared towards suppressing the Christian worldview. They do so, seeking to prove that they are a company committed to *real* equality and diversity. Thus, calls for tolerance become calls to silence Christians. This silencing of believers gives those who are opposed to Christianity a greater voice not only on matters of diversity but, sadly, also on matters regarding what is to be considered truth.

Multiculturalism, then, is the blueprint of the world's ideas and methods for pursuing racial and cultural unity. They identified the problem to be intolerance and built a solution to that problem by pushing tolerance as the supreme truth and goal. Yet, there is much in the story of contextualization, which proves how futile and empty it became precisely because it did not allow the biblical Word of God to summon it to its task and to judge the results.[74] This is the culture in which the church is called to minister and find its way in fighting for true harmony among brothers and sisters of different races.

The need to highlight the centrality of the cross in pursuing racial harmony is owing to the fact that our culture is pursuing unity at the expense of the cross. As saints of old were more influenced by culture than the cross on the issue of race, we must give attention to the stability of our thinking. We must be certain that we are biblical in our thinking, practice, and pursuit, rather than reflecting the erroneous notions of multiculturalism.

Our contribution to racial harmony must be to bring the gospel to center stage so that Christ can display His grand, harmonizing power to the world. The world can follow suit or be crushed, but for the Christian, the cross must be the central reference point upon which the wheels of our methodology spin. We need to think in terms of a Christian worldview, where truth is not relative but universally binding upon all people.

Every cultural norm and religious belief must find its validity in relationship to the cross of Christ. If a belief opposes the gospel, it must be denied. If a cultural norm dethrones Christ, it must be rejected. Our worldview must be supremely and chiefly cross-centered. In dealing with competing worldviews in his own day, Paul wrote these words to the church at Corinth regarding the standard by which all truth claims should be judged:

> *For though we walk in the flesh, we are not waging warfare according to the flesh. For the weapons of our warfare are not of the flesh but have divine power to destroy strongholds. We destroy arguments and every lofty opinion raised against the knowledge of God, and take every thought captive to obey Christ ....* — **2 Corinthians 10:3-5**

Paul clearly sees the nature of our warfare, which he describes as "destroying strongholds," to be that which takes place in the realm of the mind. He uses words such as "arguments," "opinion," and "thought."

Christians must be thinking people whose minds are centered on the gospel. We must be people who not only believe in Christ and the Bible but understand its invasive power in all of our living. The warfare imaged here is that which seeks to invade the soul of the believer being targeted by the world on a daily basis. Moment by moment, it seems, we are challenged to think differently about truth and, therefore, to think differently about the nature and pursuit of racial unity.

We must, however, remain vigilant in contending against the cultural impositions upon our thinking and fight such attempts to place strongholds on our opinions, thoughts, and arguments. We do this by putting every argument up against the truth of the Word of God. Since all of history centers on Christ—the Old Testament anticipates His work, and the New Testaments explains His work—all truth claims will be consistent with the singular glory of Christ.

The pursuit of racial harmony is not merely looking forward in hope of achieving something (though we anticipate the fullness of it as described in Revelation 5:9). It is living in light of the reality that such harmony has already been accomplished in the life and death of Christ, symbolized by the cross.

The Power of the Cross in the Pursuit of Racial Harmony

The cross of Jesus Christ is both symbolic of the pain and agony that are the consequences of our sin and God's wrath and expressive of the triumph of God over our sin through His wrath poured out upon the sinless Christ. Christ, in that one event, made a spectacle of such forces and thereby achieved peace for the elect in Him.

When we consider the actions of God in redeeming His people from sin, we see the power of the cross to unite people of different colors and cultures in two significant events: the Tower of Babel and Pentecost. In Genesis 11, we see the dispersing of mankind from Babel into all the places of the earth. This dispersion came as the rebuke of God because men sought to command their own destinies, saying,

Come, let us build ourselves a city and a tower with its top in the heavens, and let us make a name for ourselves, lest

we be dispersed over the face of the whole earth. —
Genesis 11:4

Out of this dispersion came nations, cultures, and the myriad of colors representative of all of humanity.

Mankind, once a single, monocultural unit, were scattered because of their pride and desire to ascend to the heavens. They were divided, and the one culture became many cultures, because of this one event of pride and rebellion. Into this darkness of division, God would speak as He had done in speaking into the dark abyss and creating the world. He would speak to this darkness and confusion caused by sin and re-create. We find in the scope of redemptive history the intervention of God into this confused division of Babel.

God intervenes by the outpouring of His Holy Spirit on the day of Pentecost in Acts 2. On that day, we see what theologians call "the administration of the Holy Spirit." He initiates His redeeming work by falling upon the disciples and causing them to speak in the tongues of the nations that were gathered together. What we are witnessing is not simply the beginning of the administration of the Holy Spirit but the wonderful, gracious act of the Lord gathering the scattered nations together.

This did not happen under some common social cause or in tolerating everyone's opinion. It happened with the hearing of the gospel, the preaching of the cross of Christ! The people were scattered in Genesis 11 because of their attempts to command their own destinies, but now the nations are united under the gospel to a divine destination: oneness in Christ.

I love the reality of this fact because it indicates that there is a thread that connects the Old Testament to the New Testament, demonstrating that God is not a God who acts differently in different dispensations. His plan is consistent, and His purpose of redemption through the crucified Messiah was always the eternal and divine design.

That God has always designed redemption to include the nations is clear from the Scriptures, and no one book in the Bible better demonstrates this connection between the triumph of the cross of Christ and racial harmony than the book of Ephesians. In it, our cosmic reconciliation back to God through Christ is the framework for the practical expression of unity and harmony in the church. It is the central theme in this letter. A bird's-eye of view of Ephesians evidences certain truths concerning racial harmony.

Salvation by election negates claims of cultural and biological superiority (Ephesians 1:3-5; 2:10). Racial harmony is established in the cross of Christ (Ephesians 2:14). Racial harmony is the visible manifestation of the glory of God (Ephesians 3:8-10, 21). Racial harmony is made a visible reality when we put off the old and put on the new (Ephesians 4:1-3, 17-32). Racial harmony means loving like Christ loved and, because of this, being lights of the world (Ephesians 5:1-14). Racial harmony, if it is to be a reality, will mean declaring war with anything that opposes its being actualized in our hearts and churches.

The aim of Paul in this epistle is to show the formation of the church (chapters 1-3) and the function of the church (chapters 4-6). Both the formation and the function are centered on the reality of the redemptive work of God in and through Christ at the cross. All that we are and must be in the church and world finds its starting point at the achievements of the cross. Every type of unity of the church is a cross-wrought unity, and Paul desires to show how this has been the divine intention of God from the very beginning.

The cross is no plan B of God. It is at the center of the divine plan and purposes of God in the world through a unified church. Ephesians 2 represents the essence of how this would be accomplished:

> *For he himself is our peace, who has made us both one and has broken down in his flesh the dividing wall of hostility by abolishing the law of commandments and ordinances, that he might create in himself one new man in place of the two, so making peace, and might reconcile us both to God in one body through the cross, thereby killing the hostility.*
> — *Ephesians 2:14-16*

The cross is the means of unity, racial and otherwise. Therefore, unity is not something that we seek to make happen; rather, it is something that we fight to maintain as an expressed reality of the power of the cross (Ephesians 4:3).

It is here that some have erred in writing and working to create something that has already been established in the cross. This is a crucial point because it dictates not only the terminology we use in speaking about racial harmony but also the methodology employed in its pursuit. We do not work for unity as if it is something we create. We work to maintain the unity already established by the cross of Christ.

This idea of maintaining demands a reorientation of the centrality of the cross in the lives and hearts of the people of God. Before racial harmony is a program or pursuit, it is a radical reorientation of our hearts and minds around the cross and its achievements. In this section of Ephesians, Paul wants us to recognize that the singular event of the cross actually achieved something for Jew and Gentile that all of history could not.

The cross achieved peace in the midst of historically opposed peoples whose hearts were steeped and rooted in philosophical, social, and religious hostility. This unity achieved through the cross was the mystery of God, hidden from all generations, until the life and death of Jesus Christ. God, in the cross of Christ, was making out of the two groups of people—Jew and Gentile—one man, one people, for His glory in the world. What all of history could not do, God accomplished in one singular event: the cross of Christ.

Whatever the hostility was, it was demolished by the reality of what Christ achieved on the cross for those who would believe. This should not land softly on us. While Paul is speaking of Jew and Gentile division, the implications are real and true for racial division in our day.

We live in a day that remains filled with racial hatred and violence such that one can scarcely tell that we have made any progress at all! Whether it be the racial tensions expressed during the 2008 presidential campaign of President Barack Obama, the death of Trajon Martin, or the Kentucky church that denied membership to an interracial couple, the reality is that we stand in need of the corrections of the cross.

J. Daniel Hays, in his book *From Every People and Nation*, helps us to see how this text has implications for us today:

> Nowhere is this theology more important for modern Christians than in dealing with *racial hostility*. Christians of other races are part of us, and divisions cannot be allowed to continue. The racial barrier is like a festering wound in the body of Christ.... The perversion of both active and passive racism must be challenged and stopped.... Racism in any form is prohibited by the equality of all people before God and by his unrestricted love. But the theology of the body of Christ deals with the issue at another level. The point is not merely that all Christians are *equal*; rather, the point is that all Christians have been *joined*, which has far more significance and impact.[75]

Our significance is not rooted in our being equal but in our being joined. Equality is not a helpful term because in the world it demands "sameness," but this is not what we are after as Christians. In fact, the reality that we are not the same is what makes the church powerful for all who are a part of it. I am better because I am not the same as everyone else, and everyone else is better because they are not like everyone else. Thus, we mean something different when we say "equality," and I think Hays is right to shift our focus to being joined.

In this way, the value of every member of the church should not be based on being like or equal to everyone else. This breeds exclusion by assimilation. Rather, our value to one another is based on the fact that we are joined to each other in Christ. This has tremendous practical implications. For example, if you are hindered, then I, being joined to you, am hindered. If you encounter restrictions, then I am restricted as well. If you are the victim of an injustice, then I am a victim of injustice.

When we experience and live out our being joined together in Christ, we are compelled to fight for one another and to stand with one another. The cross does not make us equal in skill, giftedness, status, or employment. It does, however, join us together so that our oneness becomes more than mere words. It is expressed in our relating to, caring for, and serving one another.

The challenge before every Christian is to maintain a cross-centered view of race relations in society and the church. As stated earlier, there is a great need for the church to think biblically about this issue and to understand all of life from a cross-centered point of view. I want to offer three implications of a cross-centered worldview that should govern our thinking and acting in our pursuit of racial harmony in the church.

Practical Implications of the Cross-Centered View of Life

People need to be compelled not by persuasive speech but by the Word of God and its implications.

The Apostle Paul, addressing the schism within the church at Corinth, goes at the heart of their problem, which was their disunity based on affirming one person over another:

> *For it has been reported to me by Chloe's people that there is quarreling among you, my brothers. What I mean is that each one of you says, "I follow Paul," or "I follow Apollos," or "I follow Cephas," or "I follow Christ." Is Christ divided? — 1 Corinthians 1:11-13*

The irony in this is that some even concluded that they were of Christ when all were of Christ. This speaks to the foolishness of division within the body of Christ. If we are all of Christ by faith, it is nonsense to speak of being divided since the Son of God is not divided. Paul speaks to this issue by taking them to the cross and declaring that the message of the cross is "to those who are called, both Jews and Greeks, ... the power of God and the wisdom of God" (1 Corinthians 1:24).

They are *called.* This is why the cross is the basis of unity. It is the message of God to the elect. It is the calling of God to those who were chosen from the foundation of the world. Paul brings in the cross and shows its centrality to their unity because, in his own words,

Christ did not send me to baptize but to preach the gospel, and not with words of eloquent wisdom, lest the cross of Christ be emptied of its power. — *1 Corinthians 1:17*

He says in another place:

And I, when I came to you, brothers, did not come proclaiming to you the testimony of God with lofty speech or wisdom. For I decided to know nothing among you except Jesus Christ and him crucified ... and my message were not in plausible words of wisdom, but in demonstration of the Spirit and of power, that your faith might not rest in the wisdom of men but in the power of God. — *1 Corinthians 2:1-3, 5*

Paul addresses the problem of disunity among the Corinthians by pointing them to the reality of the achievement of God in the cross. He is more concerned with their being compelled by the power of the gospel than the wisdom of man. The goal in calling for racial harmony in the body of Christ is not to be the one who persuades people to its necessity but the one who points to and proclaims the gospel, that men may be moved by the wisdom of God and not man.

A man or church that is moved to pursue racial harmony because of the gospel will persevere in this pursuit. For this reason, we must not seek to persuade on the basis of reason or cultural norms but by the wisdom of God, which is displayed in the cross of Christ. When someone is persuaded to pursue racial harmony because of its being rooted in the gospel and grace, no one will be able to persuade him or her otherwise. Though there will be battles of belief and conscience, the reality is that the heart won by the cross will be the heart that moves with the cross.

If you were to take a poll of any evangelical church in the country and ask whether or not pursuing racial harmony was a good thing, you would probably receive an overwhelming "yes." Why is it, then, that racial exclusion is still an issue in evangelical churches, even among those who would agree that it is a problem that needs to be addressed? In his book *A Dream Deferred*, Shelby Steele writes,

> *[O]ften people do not listen as much for the truth as for the necessity that will hold them accountable to the truth.*[76]

While Steele writes from a secular perspective, there is truth in the statement that makes it useful for our discussion.

There are many Christians who believe that racial harmony is something worth pursuing, but the thing that keeps some from actually pursuing it is that they have not yet found that which holds them accountable to do something. The call of all in the church is to keep the cross the main issue in racial harmony. If men can be shown the moral connection between life in the Body and their belief in Christ, men might feel compelled to make racial harmony a necessary pursuit in their life. The challenge, then, is not to be cute, novel, or charismatic. The goal is to compel people by and through the very gospel they claim to believe. This is what Paul did in his confrontation with Peter (Galatians 2:11-14).

According to Paul, Peter stood "condemned" (Galatians 2:11) and was acting "hypocritically" (Galatians 2:13), and this was because Peter's "conduct was not in step with the truth of the gospel" (Galatians 2:14). When men are made to see these gospel connections, only then will racial harmony truly become an issue of the heart. Peter was condemned because he refused to eat with Gentiles, and Paul said that such behavior was inconsistent with the gospel. The same is true of actions that refuse to pursue racial harmony. If Christians can see the role of the cross in our internal relations with one another in the Bible and still walk away feeling justified in not pursuing racial harmony, they stand opposed to the implications of what it means to be a Christian.

We must assume that within redeemed humanity, there resides the ability to love beyond earthly measure.

This is a difficult aspect of pursuing racial harmony because it is the one that cuts right to the place of the problem: our hearts. Without a cross-centered perspective on life and reality, we are not able to live out this dynamic of the cross in Christian relationships.

This particular rationale was birthed out of a comment related to America's differing perception, opinion, and affection with respect to Martin Luther King, Jr., and Malcolm X. It is clear that Martin Luther King, Jr., has a place in America that Malcolm X never had. It was not until the release of the movie *X* by Spike Lee that even some blacks formed a different view of Malcolm. Why is it that people have differing perceptions of these men? It lies in the fact that King assumed an innocence among whites that Malcolm did not. King believed that even though whites were behaving in ways that were evil and treating blacks as less than human, they possessed an ability to love beyond what they were demonstrating.

Early Malcolm, however, held that whites were acting according to their nature, which was of the devil, and, therefore, did not conceive of them being able to be anything different from what they had demonstrated. I refer to "early" Malcolm because it became clear that while his religious affiliation did not change, his views concerning whites and his willingness to work with them and they with him changed to being open rather than exclusive.

The cross is the voice of God to those redeemed by the blood of Christ, which says that Christians are able to behave, live, and love beyond what we may currently express. If some treat us with contempt, say things that are evil to us, or behave in ways that are inappropriate, we must believe that if the Spirit of the Lord dwells within them, He is able to cause a Christ-like love to abound in their hearts.

I have expressed the heart of this point in this little rhyme: "Romans 7 is for all who are going to heaven." In this chapter, Paul writes these often-quoted words:

For we know that the law is spiritual, but I am of the flesh, sold under sin. I do not understand my own actions. For I do not do what I want, but I do the very thing I hate. Now if I do what I do not want, I agree with the law, that it is good. So now it is no longer I who do it, but sin that dwells within me. For I know that nothing good dwells in me, that is, in my flesh. For I have the desire to do what is right, but not the ability to carry it out. For I do not do the good I want, but the evil I do not want is what I keep on doing. Now if I do what I do not want, it is no longer I who do it, but sin that dwells within me.

So I find it to be a law that when I want to do right, evil lies close at hand. For I delight in the law of God, in my inner being, but I see in my members another law waging war against the law of my mind and making me captive to the law of sin that dwells in my members. Wretched man that I am! Who will deliver me from this body of death? Thanks be to God through Jesus Christ our Lord! So then, I myself serve the law of God with my mind, but with my flesh I serve the law of sin. — **Romans 7:14-25**

We all love this passage in Romans because it reminds us that our struggle with sin is the very life of genuine Christianity.

It is not wrong to battle sin. In fact, the battle is a distinguishing mark of true faith. The teaching of Paul, however, applies not simply to us personally but to all who claim Christ and truly know Him as Lord and Savior. Therefore, we must extend its teaching and implications to all of our relationships, black or white.

For instance, one time I snapped at my wife in one of those moments when we were engaged in *intense fellowship*. When the smoke cleared and the time of apology came, the first thing that I wanted her to know, even before I apologized, was this: "What I did, honey, I did not mean to do. In fact, I did not even *want* to do it. I did it because of the sin that is within me!" Well, I did not say it exactly like that, but I did appeal to Romans 7 for defense. It did not work, by the way.

Here is the point. In all of my appeals to her on the basis of indwelling sin and in all of my longings for her to see the battle of my soul, the real question is this: When she does wrong, will I see and apply the teaching of Romans 7 to her? The fact of the matter is that it does apply to her even though I am not inclined to do so. The sad truth is that when she appeals to Romans 7, I have often held up the standard of perfection.

In other words, I do not remember all of my appeals to Romans 7; rather, my mind goes straight to the law, and my heart wants to be justified in its anger. I treat her as if she should have acted or responded with perfect holiness when, in fact, she was having a Romans 7 moment. Romans 7 is for all who are going to heaven!

Here is the implication. When I am wronged or feel wronged, whether it is true or not, if I desire God to be glorified in and through my pursuit of racial harmony, my response must be in accordance with this desire. I must temper my response by reminding myself that the person who has wronged me is able to act in ways more godly than what he or she displayed.

This should be our posture, not because the brother has this capability within himself but because the same Holy Spirit who is at work in me, sanctifying me and making me more like Christ, is at work in him as well. Even when people speak or behave in ways that exclude or seem prejudiced, the cross teaches me to treat them based on what God can do in them and not what they have done or said.

As we pray for God to be working a Christ-like ability to love in the hearts of our fellow Christians, we must also pray that God would be doing the same within us. If we would have men and women be changed in this area of racial exclusion and live as those who love beyond earthly measure, we must model what we desire others to be. We must assume that while they are not what they should be—as none of us are—they are, by grace, moving in that direction. This is not an easy thing to do.

The truth is that God never gives commands that are easy because every command demands a power outside of us. I am not writing as one who has been perfect in this, either. I write as one whose heart had to be saved many times from bitterness and frustrations, from the dominance of culture above Christ. I am certain that the future will afford me more opportunities to grow in Christ-like love.

Relationships are hard by themselves, and when you add the cross-cultural element, the difficulty increases because the possibility of offense heightens. For this reason, many have walked away from the pursuit of racial harmony. I believe it was because they failed to apply this sanctifying implication of the gospel: Romans 7 is for all who go to heaven.

Others have walked away because they have grown tired of not being understood or, when misunderstood, not having the opportunity to explain themselves and their genuine intentions. Fighting for a cross-centered perspective on racial harmony will, without a doubt, be one of the most difficult things you do. The difficulty is a gift, though, because its weight shifts our gaze from our own strength and power to that which has been procured for us in the death of our Lord upon the cross: the power of the Holy Spirit. The strength of seeing Christ in others when their words or actions look otherwise is the strength provided by a cross-centered worldview.

The issues surrounding racial harmony—justice and forgiveness—are chiefly cross issues.

The cross of Christ teaches us that we are to be men and women who are committed to the high and virtuous issues of justice and forgiveness. Both are chiefly and most gloriously displayed in the cross.

It has been stated by many proponents of racial harmony that the polarization of race in the church is demonstrated in the view that each gives to the representation of the cross. Whites, for instance, tend to see the cross as a symbol of victory and triumph, whereas African Americans would identify with the pain and the agony behind the cross. While there may be exceptions to this, it does represent the diverse perspectives of the cross to believers.

The irony is that the triumph of the cross is the triumph for any African American believer and the pain of the cross is for every White believer. We are all, however, tempted to see everything in the light of our present cultural realities. Blacks will highlight the justice aspect of the cross and the fact that the oppressor, the devil, was vanquished by the power of God. That which seemed to triumph—the death and, seeming, oppression of Christ on the cross—was soon overthrown by the justice of God in the death and resurrection of Jesus. Triumph, then, is what is hoped for. For blacks, the present realities, perceived or real, of pain and agony are the dynamics in which they find identification with the cross.

This is nothing new, however, in the African American culture. The pain of the cross and the eventual triumph that was its result have filled the writings of this people, nowhere better expressed than in the "negro spirituals." These were more than the songs of the people. They represented the heart and hopes of the people, and many of the songs were filled with a justice and deliverance motif.[77]

Right through the Civil Rights era, blacks have sought to root their hope in songs of freedom. The marches were called "freedom marches," and some who rode from city to city for the cause of justice were called "freedom riders." This was because at the root of African American existence was their battle to overcome that which had been denied but longed for: freedom. This longing stemmed from the reality that they were made in the image of God and bondage was inconsistent with their natural and God-given freedom, which they now felt more keenly in their being born again.

The danger that can come from this view, however, is the belief of victimology. Singing songs of the slaves today paints a picture that is not true of our current culture. Freedom has come in Christ, and as citizens of the United States, we must recognize measures of progress. This being so, some of the historical situations that produced the spirituals of old songs are not evident today.

What can occur, then, with such a preoccupation with this kind of freedom is viewing whites today the way they were viewed in the past. Not only this, but some blacks can find justification to feel that the reason they are not successful or have not attained the American dream is because of what whites have and are continuing to do. This one-sided focus of the cross, therefore, is dangerous.

With respect to the triumphant view of the cross, whites focus on what the cross has achieved. This focused view has its own potential dangers. It can cause many who embrace it to use it as a means of diversion rather than sincerity. This view of the cross as a symbol of victory can cause some not to identify or feel empathy with those whose situations in life are less than victorious. It can produce a critical rather than caring spirit.

For instance, when cries of injustice are made, some whites have difficulty in drawing near to those who cry out, not out of disinterest but simply out of the inability to identify. When they are faced with the realities of injustice in the world and in the church, they deal with it by highlighting the forgiveness of wrongs, calling the oppressed to forgiveness as opposed to the oppressor to repentance. It is not that the wrongs are dismissed so much as it is an inability to feel what it means to need freedom and victory.

The interpretation of the history of our country has come from the minds of those who have known victory. Thus, history books are riddled with a sense of American greatness even in the chapters that deal with the less than honorable aspects of our history. They only know victory and, thus, tragedy is contextualized in victorious terms.

When we consider these different perspectives of the cross, we are able to grasp the different rally cries of blacks and whites. The rally cry for blacks is: "We want freedom!" The rallying cry of whites is: "We want forgiveness." There is a problem, however, with both views of reality. It is not that they are not looking at the cross—they are! The problem is that both groups' understanding of the cross pits justice and forgiveness against one another. This dichotomy promotes views of the cross that are defined by our culture rather than the Bible. We desperately need to see what the gospel demands.

D. A. Carson is helpful when he says:

[Whites] need to get on their knees and read Amos; [blacks] need to get down on their knees and read 1 Peter. All of us need to return to the cross. For the cross teaches us that if all we ask for is justice, we are all damned; it teaches us that God himself is passionately interested in forgiveness and its price. That is why we cannot expect such responses from large swaths of secular society, whose categories for redressing social evils, real and perceived, lie elsewhere. Among Christians to expect anything less is to betray the faith.[78]

At the cross, we see both justice and forgiveness expressed, and our understanding of both must find their origin in the divine intention of the cross.

Jesus came and suffered so that we might have a pattern for our suffering. This pattern in Jesus keeps us from seeing suffering as something that is inconsistent with victory. He rose victorious not only so the disenfranchised could hope but also that, by His example, they might see and embrace the reality that suffering and victory are twins. Christ's suffering was, in large measure, His victory.

Whatever way one views the cross, it stands as the reminder of the wrath and the forgiveness of God. It compels Christians to look deeper than what can be seen and to listen for more than what can merely be heard. In the wood of the cross, we see more than wood. We see the sovereign design of God. In the echoes of the cross, we hear more than mere voices. We hear the reverberating words of our Savior: "It is finished."

In those words, we do not hear the end of life but, rather, the end of sin. We do not hear the last words of our Lord; we hear the last sound of temporal and cultural divisions. "It is finished" are more than words signaling the end of the events of the cross. They are words that declare the achievement of the cross. Christ has finished the work that God sent Him to do, and that work was to glorify God by making a people for Himself out of every nation.

Herein is the challenge of this chapter: Will we live out a cross-centered interpretation of unity, or will we live through our culture's varied expressions of what it should be and how to attain it? Which will it be, the cross or culture? It surely cannot be both. May God grant us the grace to live in the achievement of the cross.

Chapter 5 Notes

_____

_____

_____

_____

_____

_____

_____

_____

_____

_____

_____

_____

_____

_____

_____

_____

_____

_____

_____

_____

CHAPTER SIX

Forget
How Blacks Work and Fight for Racial Harmony

We are all men and women of history. Some love to study it while others run as far away from it as they can. The reality is that we cannot and do not escape it. We make it, use it, and live it every day. As believers in Jesus Christ, it is only logical that we love history since the very essence of our life and faith, the Bible, is a first-century document.

History is what drives and governs our present actions and attitudes and our future plans. History, then, is a wonderful tool for all who will give themselves to it. Yet, as beautiful and necessary as it is, when it comes to the history of racial tensions in America, it becomes extremely divisive in the world and, sadly, within the church. It is without dispute that this is our history and that our present racial tensions are rightly understood only in the context of that history.

If racial harmony is to become a reality within the church, we must be careful not to conclude that history does not matter or that history is all that matters. While there are measures of truth in each of these statements, each by itself is dangerous. We must be careful not to spiritualize away the facts of history but remain ready and willing to do the hard work of dealing with it and its present-day implications.

It is worth noting here that it is precisely because of this factor of history that I use the racial tension between blacks and whites as the paradigm for the principle of this chapter. This is not to exclude the reality that there are tensions across many racial and cultural fronts. However, due to the factors concerning the brutality of slavery, the legalized continuation of the same in Jim Crowism, and the cruel realities of rape, lynchings, and a host of other dehumanizing actions, one must admit that there is not a tension as pronounced as that which exists between blacks and whites.

American culture has not escaped the reality of her history. Even those within the church who are products of that history are affected, some being crippled by the staggering effects of its known yet seemingly elusive character. For the believers in Jesus Christ, however, ours is a radical call. It is our understanding of God that must govern us and not the realities of American history, the country's present dilemmas, or our culture. How we understand anything and everything must be governed and shaped by our understanding of God's redemptive and sovereign rule in and through every event of history.

This means that Christians stand in a unique place of looking back on history and being able to view it from a totally renewed and redeemed understanding of God's sovereignty within it. As we contemplate and converse about this issue of racial harmony and racial exclusion within and without the church, we must not look through the lenses provided to us by our sin and culture, which darken our understanding. Rather, we have been given new eyes and new hearts through regeneration, and it is with these that we are to view and understand history.

The path to this disposition, however, is not easy. I call it a path because racial harmony is a journey to living out what God has already made us in Christ. It is a journey with all of the trappings of danger, misunderstanding, confusion, and offense. It is not something that is quick and easy. It is not something that can be achieved with a stadium event or a two-day seminar. It will be a burden, but it will be a joyful burden as we see the beauty of God from the backdrop of our sin and arrogance.

Racial harmony, then, is a challenge and call to take a radically different look at history in order to shape our views, understandings, and actions in the present. In 1997, in an attempt to make sense of how to begin tackling the racial tensions that exist within the church, the phrase "forget and remember" came to me. I believe that this was a gift from the Holy Spirit. Since that time, this phrase has served as a paradigm in which this process of unity could begin. I have used it in various settings, including conferences and seminars, and found that many have been helped by it and their faith nurtured as they reflected and sought to apply these two necessary action points: forget and remember.

The reason this paradigm has proven helpful for many over the years is due to its gospel-centered focus. To forget and to remember are challenges that call us to make sense of the realities of history through the lens of the gospel. From that position, we are helped in our understanding as well as in our disposition in dealing with the present difficulties of exclusion in our lives and our churches. This is important because dealing with the challenges of exclusion today always leads both sides to discussions of history.

Blacks suggest that the present acts of exclusion are the result of a slanted interpretation of history. Whites seek to focus on the progress that has occurred over the decades. This, some blacks suggest, is an attempt to leave behind the horrors of history, which as a consequence, minimizes the difficulties of the present. This difference in perception of the same reality has been a major stumbling block in the church's discussions and progress in this area of racial harmony.

The challenge of the gospel to forget is not to forget the facts of history but, rather, to reinterpret history with a gospel-centered focus. It is to see history with new eyes and to relate to one another in the present with new hearts. Both new eyes and a new heart are fruits of regeneration. The pursuit of racial harmony is first within our own hearts and then in our churches. This calls for something radical, something which can be produced only by the Holy Spirit and sustained by our hard work as well as His effectual work in and through us.

To that end, the challenge of this and the next chapter is for blacks and whites to view history through the lens of the gospel. To do this means that blacks need to forget and whites need to remember. Blacks, because of their commitment to the gospel and its fruit, are called to forget history and its atrocities. Whites, because of their commitment to the gospel and its fruits, are called to remember the past and to acknowledge its current effects, psychological, social, and otherwise, on both blacks and whites.

Blacks Need to Forget

When I say that African Americans must forget history, the term "forget" has always raised eyebrows. Some are reading this book and at this point are tempted to put it down, believing me to be a bit insane. A little explanation, however, will calm the fury. The call to forget history means to forget in the sense that our attitudes and our relationships with believers of different cultures should not be governed or dictated by the past.

The realities of slavery, Jim Crowism, and the battles of the Civil Rights era must not be the filters through which we deal with present injustices. This is not to suggest that we turn a deaf ear to the familiar slurs or continual acts of exclusion or injustice. Rather, our response to such things must be filtered through the understanding of God's sovereignty and the dual lenses of grace and forgiveness. Again, we must have a gospel-centered perspective.

Sometimes, but not always, our hurts, anger, and feelings of pain can be the result of a wrong focus. The pain and hurt are real, but when these hurts are allowed to brew, we are compelled to respond in ways that may not be healthy or Christ-like. The gospel challenges our actions as well as the motivations of our hearts to see with new eyes and from a new perspective, a perspective that is rooted in the sovereign design of God and His purpose and plan in every event of our lives and history.

The Apostle Paul commands the following when we are offended:

> *Repay no one evil for evil.... Do not be overcome by evil, but overcome evil with good.* — **Romans 12:17, 21**

Do not let the evil tendencies of men move you to behave in ways that are consistent with evil. Paul's challenge not to render evil for evil is not only a challenge to the actions of men but one that extends to the heart of a man.

There have been times when I have been grieved by others over racial matters and have verbally stated my forgetting of the matter. Yet, in my heart, not only was the wound still fresh but so, too, was the attitude of anger and resentment. This was because I let my heart and mind justify my feelings of resentment by filtering the offense through the lens of history, not the gospel. I was allowing my flesh to think negatively, and I would say to myself, "Things have not changed at all," or "This is why you cannot trust them, Sherard." This is not the kind of forgetting that the gospel moves us to embrace and express. The gospel challenges me to a deeper level of forgetting, a forgetting that touches, moves, and changes. It is not only what I say about an offense that matters but what I feel about it.

A biblical precedent for this is found in the parable of the unforgiving servant in Matthew 18:21-35. In the last verse of this parable, Jesus commands a forgiveness that is not simply one of a stated proposition but one of affection: "So also my heavenly Father will do to every one of you, if you do not forgive your brother from your heart" (Matthew 18:35). Where there is no heart forgiveness, head forgiveness is not sufficient to model Christ-like forgiveness.

At this point, I must hasten to clarify what I am not saying in this call to forget. Two specific things are not intended here. The first is that I do not mean that we should forget in the cognitive sense of the term. I am not calling blacks to forget history by acting as if it never happened. This is, of course, impossible, and it also would be an offense to God, the Creator and Lord of every event of history. As a black man, I love my history, and my hope is that we never lose sight of it. Since God is the Maker of history and since anything that He creates is good, to act as if something God has made can and should be discarded or denied is spiritually and practically unwise.

Second, I do not intend to establish or promote a false dichotomy that sets forgetting over or against the pursuit of justice. Volf is very helpful here in his assessment of forgiveness. He writes,

> Forgiveness is no mere discharge of a victim's angry resentment and no mere assuaging of a perpetrator's remorseful anguish, one that demands no change of the perpetrator and no righting of wrongs. On the contrary: every act of forgiveness enthrones justice; it draws attention to its violation precisely by offering to forego its claims.... Only those who are forgiven and who are willing to forgive will be capable of relentlessly pursuing justice without falling into the temptation to pervert it into injustice....[79]

When I speak of blacks forgetting, what I have in mind is the essence of what it means to forgive. The call to forget is the challenge of forgiveness. Forgetting is the radical call to assess and address the real actions and words that promote racial inequities and injustices through the matrix of God-like forgiveness.

I use the phrase "God-like forgiveness" because Christians never demonstrate the character of God in this racial conundrum more than when we demonstrate His kind of forgiveness. God's forgiveness is on display when we forget the sins of the past and the present because of what we believe about God, Christ, sin, and the cross. These truths of the gospel must, by the grace of the Holy Spirit, work deep within us a cross-centeredness that guides and governs our perceptions and definitions of reality.

Forgetting is God-like because in its essence, it models God's forgiveness of our offense towards Him.

When we mine the pages of Scripture, we find a God whose very basis of salvation is owing to His forgetting our sin. As with our forgetting, I do not intend here a cognitive forgetting on God's part, either. I want to be clear here. God's knowledge is full, complete, and exhaustive. It is this reality of His knowledge that makes His forgiveness even more glorious and instructive to us. That God forgets does not mean that He lacks knowledge of events. He forgets in the sense that, while He is very aware of our sins and the intentions of our hearts (Genesis 6:5), He chooses not to deal with us according to our sin. This is precisely the reason why David calls his soul to "bless the Lord" and this with a double emphasis:

> Bless the LORD, O my soul, and all that is within me, bless his holy name! Bless the LORD, O my soul, and forget not all his benefits.... He does not deal with us according to our sins, nor repay us according to our iniquities. For as high as the heavens are above the earth, so great is his steadfast love toward those who fear him; as far as the east is from the west, so far does he remove our transgressions from us. — *Psalm 103:1-2, 10-12*

To forget, therefore, is not the lack of knowledge regarding an offense but the active choice to forgive in the full knowledge of the offense. It is to choose not to deal with the offender on the basis of the offense. It means to make the choice not to give the offender what he or she deserves (justice as we see it) but instead to give the offender what he or she does not deserve, which is mercy!

To respond this way is gospel-centered because it is to act as God did in and through Christ. God does not forget in the sense that He acts as if there were no offense at all to be dealt with. Rather, God's forgetting is the act of His forgiveness. The knowledge of the offense moves the cross-centered man or woman to respond in acts of mercy and forgiveness as God does. This is exactly why this kind of response, forgetting, is God-like.

Let's consider this in another way. To forget is another way of saying to forgive, and forgiveness necessitates offense. This bears deeper consideration than is our purpose here, but consider that truth: if there were no offense, forgiveness would be unnecessary. We can speak of forgiveness with great clarity and insight, yet when it is called for, it can still be the hardest thing to give. This is because, in some respect, while we can describe forgiveness, we sometimes fail to consider the fact that forgiveness needs an offense in order to exist. What makes it even more challenging is the reality that the greater the offense, the more difficult it is to forgive but the more necessary forgiveness becomes.

Thus, in all of our being offended, we must remind ourselves that God, the Creator of all things, is the most offended being in the universe. Still, He forgave the vilest of offenders. He alone has the right to deal with us according to our sin, and whatever He does is just and fair. But the wonder of it all is that He chooses something very different. He acts in the opposite way. Not only does God not seek to deal with us according to our sin and repay us for our infinite offenses against His glory and majesty, but He also works to remove the offense: "as far as the east is from the west, so far does he remove our transgressions from us" (Psalm 103:12). The prophet Isaiah put it this way:

> *I, I am he who blots out your transgressions for my own sake, and I will not remember your sins.* — **Isaiah 43:25**

God's forgetting, then, is not His acting as if there were no sin. Sin and offense had to be dealt with.

Herein is the beauty of the gospel and the grounds of our being forgiven by God: He chose to deal with our sin in the crushing of His Son, Jesus Christ.

> *But he was pierced for our transgressions; he was crushed for our iniquities; upon him was the chastisement that brought us peace, and with his wounds we are healed.... Yet it was the will of the LORD to crush him; he has put him to grief; when his soul makes an offering for guilt, he shall see his offspring; he shall prolong his days; the will of the LORD shall prosper in his hand.* — **Isaiah 53:5, 10**

O the beauty of this wonderful, matchless, sovereign grace of God! How deserving we are of death and hell, and yet our God, because of the Person and work of Christ on our behalf, does not simply cover our sins but blots them out! He does not forgive with a twinge of remembering; He casts our sin into the depths of the sea (Micah 7:19). This is the foundation and motivation for our forgiving the offenses of others towards us.

If the holy and just God of the universe can forgive the infinite offense from us against Him, what is your offense to me? What is my offense to you? If He can forgive my heinous sin and the daily residual effects of it, how much more can I, through Christ, forgive the varying degrees of injustice and the acts of exclusion of fellow brothers and sisters towards me? We must condition our minds through the knowledge and experience of His grace to believe and act in this God-like way when we are offended.

I must admit that every time I talk or speak in this way, my heart drops because of the tremendous ways this can and has been misunderstood by some blacks, who question my integrity as a black man, and misused by some whites, who get a misguided feeling of vindication because of my words. The misunderstandings and misuses of some, however, do not negate the powerful expression of the wonders and power of the cross for our lives in this pursuit of racial harmony.

Just as we do not deny freedoms in the Bible because some abuse and misuse them, neither do we deny this gospel requirement of forgiveness because of misunderstanding or misuse. Forgetting is not easy, but it is Christ-like and gospel-soaked living and, therefore, necessary. We must see in the difficult demands of the gospel the continual need for the power of the grace of Christ in our own lives and hearts to this end.

The need for forgiveness has been established and affirmed in this matter, but the way to do this is still lacking. Like anything that is transforming in our lives, it must begin with how and what we think. If we are to learn to forget and if this forgetting is to be a genuine, growing, and sustained affection over time, it must be rooted in three truths that we keep in the forefront of our thinking: the fact of Christ's death, the truth that saved sinners have been forgiven, and the truth that unsaved offenders will receive their due.

The Fact of Christ's Death

When men sin against us, regardless of the nature of the offense, we must keep in mind that none have offended us to the degree that we have offended God. We must keep this thought ever before us: the most offended being in the universe is God!

He created us for His own glory and fame, and all of humanity—red, yellow, black, and white—in Adam have sinned and continue to sin. While God is the most offended being in the universe, He is also the most glorious being in the universe. He is infinitely holy and worthy of infinite affection and praise, which we all have failed to give to Him. What He does receive from mankind, even redeemed humanity, is not always in keeping with the nature of His will or character.

In our great and cosmic offense, God has, by sheer sovereign mercy, chosen to forget our sin by forgiving it in, through, and because of Christ alone. When people sin against us or offend us, it is only sinners acting sinfully towards a fellow sinner. Yet, when we sin, we sin against the Holy One. The point is simple: no offense against us can compare to the offense of humanity against its Creator. If God has acted in the way of forgiveness towards sinners, how much more can and should we respond when sinned against?

In the grand scheme of all of my sin and offenses towards the Holy God, what is the offense of exclusion towards me that I cannot forgive? The gospel compels me to view the offense as an opportunity to show what it means to be one whose offense has been forgiven by God by forgiving the one who offends me. This is a gospel-centered perspective.

Saved Sinners Have Been Forgiven

When we are offended by one who professes to be a Christian, we must temper our response with this mindset: Christ has died for that sin. In other words, when a Christian sins against us and we then hold that sin against him or her, we are in danger of making a mockery of the effect of the cross.

When a brother offends us, we must ask ourselves, "What sin has Christ *not* nailed to the cross for this brother?" The answer is none! All sin, for all Christians, is done away with in the cross of Christ. Philip P. Bliss (1838-1876) captured the wonder of this achievement of the cross in the hymn "It Is Well with My Soul":

> My sin, oh the bliss of this glorious thought, my sin not in part but the whole, he has nailed to the cross, and I bear them no more; praise the Lord, praise the Lord, O my soul.

The words "I bear them no more" express the relationship of the redeemed person concerning his sin and standing before God. It also expresses why we must forgive the sin committed against us by another believer: he bears them no more.

If Christ has nailed that Christian's sin, including actions of exclusion and injustice, to the cross and he bears them no more, who am I to treat that believer as if he still bears that sin? To deal with Christians according to their sin is to behave in ways contrary to the gospel. It is to act in ways that are opposite of God's way towards us. In doing so, we act as if the achievements of the gospel for the one who offended us are null and void. To forgive an offense, we must keep in mind, at all times, that the brother who sinned against me has his sins forgiven, even that sin of racial exclusion and injustice.

We must battle against the demonic mentality that accuses where the cross has forgiven. We must seek to forgive because forgiveness, by faith in Christ, has already taken place on the brother's behalf. This does not mean that we do not talk about the offense or we act as if the offense never took place. Unity and harmony do not eliminate the need for hard discussions. They should, in these cases, take place. What it does mean is that we are not to condemn a brother for a sin from which God has delivered him. This is a gospel-centered perspective.

Unbelievers Will Receive Their Due

What we have talked about thus far is how to respond when a believer offends us. Now we give consideration to responding to unbelievers. With such persons, the achievements of the cross have not been applied; therefore, their sins remain, and they continue to bear them. With such persons, it might be a bit easier to act in ways that are unreflective of the gospel because we can justify that they "deserve it." Yet, even here, the gospel response still applies.

When the offense comes from one who is unsaved and who actively opposes the gospel, we must deal with such a person from an eternal perspective. This is what Christ did when He was reviled and persecuted, and this is the example that we must follow. The Apostle Peter said of our Lord,

> *When he was reviled, he did not revile in return; when he suffered, he did not threaten, but continued entrusting himself to him who judges justly.* — **1 Peter 2:23**

When we are persecuted, we must not seek vengeance. In the case of unbelievers, we must commend them to God, who

> *... considers it just to repay with affliction those who afflict you, and to grant relief to you who are afflicted as well as to us, when the Lord Jesus is revealed from heaven with his mighty angels.* — **2 Thessalonians 1:6, 7**

We must resist vengeance, knowing that Christ experiences the pains of our persecution (Acts 9:4) and that He will avenge His name and glory by giving our oppressors and accusers their due.

We can treat unbelievers with respect and bear their verbal and physical mistreatments because we know that vengeance belongs to the Lord and that those who oppose His children will be dealt with eternally in the last day. When these realities are in the forefront of our minds, we are enabled, through the power of the Holy Spirit, to respond in ways that make much of the gospel and glorify God. This is a gospel-centered perspective and the heart of forgetting.

What I desire in my own heart as well as in the hearts and affections of my black brothers and sisters is to be like God when we are offended by choosing to forgive. The forgiveness that ultimately matters is the forgiveness of God, and when we forgive others, we echo His forgiveness.[80] Forgetting is forgiving the most radical of offenses for the sake of the glory of God and the triumph of the gospel in our lives and in the church. Nothing is a greater challenge to my own soul in this fight than this.

Does Forgiveness Demand an Apology?

One of the challenges to forgiveness is the thinking that an apology must precede it. This makes sense, but it is not necessarily true. The execution of gospel forgiveness does not depend on an apology but may be granted, by the grace and help of God, before a word of apology is spoken. An example of forgiveness granted in the absence of apology is Christ as He hung upon the cross (Luke 23:34).

It is also confirmed in the timing of the forgiveness of Jesus for our sin, which, according to Paul, occurred while we were sinners (Romans 5:8). Not only did such an expression of love and forgiveness occur before we confessed our sin, but it is actually the foundation for our confession.

We must consider the truth that our forgiveness is the light that leads us to see the heart of another's offense towards us. Sometimes God uses our forgiveness as a means of grace to others since forgiveness frees the offender to see his or her need to offer an apology. The love of God was that light for us, showing us the depth of our offense towards Him. This is why the scripture says,

> *In this is love, not that we have loved God but that he loved us.... We love because he first loved us.* — *1 John 4:10, 19*

The fact is that if Christ had not forgiven us, we would not have seen our sin and been compelled to love Him.

In this way, we see that a major key in racial harmony is forgiveness. Unity with God could not happen until or unless the offended one, the Lord, first forgave us. Thus, the practical unity of the church cannot happen unless or until the offended first offers forgiveness. Forgiveness is the key to unity.

Chapter 6 Notes

CHAPTER SEVEN

Remember

How Whites Work and Fight for Racial Harmony

That this chapter is shorter than the previous does not suggest that the role of whites in racial harmony is less challenging or important. When I call white believers to remember, I mean that they must realize and embrace the harsh realities of history and its present residual effects. When discussions about race and racism emerge, the feeling of most whites has been one of defensiveness. The defense "I was not there when those terrible things took place" shows the desire not to be identified with those in the past that have held and perpetuated slavery and those who were defenders of segregation. The result is that when blacks begin to discuss the *present* realities of exclusion, the response of some whites is to dismiss or disregard these experiences as simply the misunderstandings of blacks who, it is presumed, are "wearing their feelings on their sleeves."

Whether this is done intentionally or unintentionally, what whites must understand is that such attitudes evince perceptions of indifference or a lack of concern for what many are experiencing in the world today. When I say that whites are to remember, like with forgetting, I do not mean, primarily, that they are to remember cognitively.

I say "primarily" because there is a sense in which the facts of history—the institution of slavery and the church's participation in it, Jim Crow, black codes, lynchings—must be known and understood. There must also be the recognition of these events as being evil, un-Christian in nature, and a significant cause for many present divisions and tensions within the church and in the world.

One of the realities in the white church has been its willful ignorance of the plight of peoples other than themselves, specifically black Americans. It appears that the white church has buried her head in the sand and has covered her ears from hearing and her eyes from seeing the historical and present cries and pains of blacks in this country. This indifference must change if the church is to be a reflection of the beauty of the gospel.

The white church must be intentional in getting out of its cultural box of comfort and carrying its cross, which, for many white Christians, may include helping people of color bear their cross. They must take hold of the mantle of justice and crush every instance of injustice in our country and the world. They must remove themselves from their position of privilege and willfully experience the pains of struggle.

This is something of what Paul meant when he said that we should "weep with those who weep" (Romans 12:15). There must be an entering into the pain and experiences of others, not with an eye on cultural imposition but with the intention of lifting, encouraging, sharing, and promoting harmony. If honesty will be a priority, many would have to admit that this kind of intentionality has not been the main way of white Christians in the past or the present.

Having said that, my chief intention in the term "remember" is something that goes beyond simple recognition. The word is sometimes used in the Bible as a covenantal term. It is used by and of God to denote something of His promise to act and behave towards an individual. When the Bible says that God remembers, it is not suggesting that God has forgotten something and then eventually remembers it. If this were the case, God would not be God. Something else is meant by this word when it relates to God.

For instance, when the Bible says that God remembered Rachel (Genesis 30:29) and Hannah (1 Samuel 1:19), it does not mean that He had forgotten about them and then, at some point, came to remember them (cognitively). Rather, at each of these points, it means that God came to the aid of these women; it means that God acted on the behalf of those who were hurting because of their circumstances or situations and were unable to help themselves.

When God remembers, it is descriptive of His actions, not His thinking. When we apply this term to how our white brothers and sisters must pursue racial harmony, it is a call to action. Historically, it was the custom of whites to turn their heads to the offenses and atrocities being suffered by African Americans.

Today, while things might differ in degree and extent from one person to the next, in principle they are still very much the same. This does not suggest that one must believe every claim of exclusion. It does mean, however, that whites fight to be quick to dismiss these claims as simply "finding exclusion under every bush." While there are, admittedly, some of whom this accusation can be made, wisdom demands that we consider a matter before we make a judgment.

Remembering is a challenge to white believers not to bury their heads in the sand and pretend that exclusion, structural and practical, does not exist. It is a call to grab hold of the biblical demands of justice and to act on the behalf of those who are treated in ways that are inconsistent with biblical virtue. Whites must step up to this challenge if the issue of racial harmony is to be more than a "black church issue."

Dwight Perry makes a helpful point to this end:

> The call to changing the way we do things must be confronted head on by those who are part of the problem— white middle-class, conservative believers. For as long as blacks and other minorities are the only ones confronting the issue, it will remain marginalized. Only when Caucasian spiritual leaders begin to exercise leadership in this area more than persons of color who live in the cycle of racism will this issue be seen as something that is legitimate.
>
> When it is not solely addressed by people of color but is aggressively addressed by those in the Caucasian

evangelical setting, the issue of racism will be seen as more than just a black issue that bitter, unforgiving blacks can't seem to recover from, but as a legitimate issue that is hurting the church.[81]

The challenge to white believers is to wake up and recognize the reality of racism and begin to engage intentionally in issues that promote justice and equality on behalf of all.

Speculation and skepticism are born out of the lack of effort to demonstrate care and concern. We must understand that the silence of many in the white church is a deafening silence. To blacks, this silence speaks loudly regarding a lack of desire for and commitment to racial harmony. Anyone not ready or willing to engage in this battle is not interested in racial harmony and, thus, not interested in the gospel. To this, the Apostle John's words are instructive to us: "let us not love in word or talk but in deed and in truth" (1 John 3:18).

Like forgetting, remembering is not easy since it requires something that goes against the grain of who we all are by nature: self-centered, ethnocentric sinners. Unfortunately, the reality of sin does not go away at conversion. It only intensifies as we seek to expel it from our hearts and minds. For whites to remember and for there to begin to be light and sight in the soul, several things must be challenged. Whites must learn to challenge undiscerning assumptions, challenge their fears, challenge white privilege, and have guts.

Challenge Undiscerning Assumptions

First, whites must learn to challenge undiscerning assumptions. Often at the root of racial division lie assumptions about people or a group of people that are unchallenged by reason or personal experience and truth. Douglas Sharp writes,

> Assumptions are the notions that we take for granted; they are the ideas, beliefs or 'facts' that are accepted as true and real without proof or demonstration. They make up the fund of common knowledge on which one draws— unreflectively and uncritically—in the course of decisions and actions, especially in interpersonal relations. The word that refers to assumptive conduct and beliefs is presumptuous, and the distance from here to *arrogance* is not far.[82]

Sharp goes on to say that when such assumptions are proved wrong, the options are obvious:

> … abandon or revise the assumption or retain it in spite of the evidence to the contrary, in which case the assumption has become prejudice and the assumer a bigot. The distance between presumption and arrogance has been effectively traversed.[83]

History has offered its way of instructing us regarding how and what to think about certain groups of people. Yet, it has done so on the basis of cultural perception of what is true about them. It is always puzzling to me when whites tell me that I am different from most that look like me. While anyone will recognize the oddity of this statement, the reality is that for most whites, because of perceptions of the black community, this is absolutely true. It is true not because I am actually different but because, having been run through the test-mill of their cultural assumptions, they find me to have experiences similar to their own. I am, therefore, "safe."

I am educated and have been to schools of which they approve. I am self-aware without possessing a victim mentality. I am articulate and have always been able to adapt to my situations. To them, I am different because their perceptions are that being black, especially a black male, means being angry and judgmental and blaming whites for everything. None of which is true.

Under their assumptions, to be black means to be inarticulate, unable to communicate effectively. It means not to value education, and within the ranks of intelligence, it certainly means to be theologically liberal in every conceivable way. I, however, passed the test.

What is a fact, however, is that every black is run through the test of the majority culture. It is not a verbal test but a visual, "let's wait and see" test. The problem is not the test per se but the measure of pass and fail, which is always based on whether or not I pass their black culture perception test.

If they were to hold the test up and view it in light of what is true, they would find that their assumptions are wrong as well as ungodly and that the distance between assumptions and arrogance is closer than they assume. Those who desire to make an impact in racial harmony must be willing to check their assumptions through personal experience and truth.

Challenge Fears

Second, whites must challenge their fears. One of the most difficult barriers to get over in the pursuit of racial harmony is that of fear. Fear of what? As one man says,

> ... fear of honest ... discovery ... confrontation ... change ... of being mistaken and ultimately ... of truth.[84]

Herein is the root of why some fear to engage in the battle. Whites are silent and seemingly indifferent because they are less desirous of the implications that may result from their being involved.

For some, this has been the constant road they have walked. In all of their efforts to build relationships and to make a difference in this area, they have been met with a suspicion that never seems to give them a way of credibility. In such cases, these persons tire of the efforts because of the inability of some blacks to move beyond perceptions. For others, however, this is not the case. Some whites never move an inch to make headway on this issue because they simply do not want to face what may be true of them.

It is like a husband whose wife says to him, "We have to talk." Every man knows what that means. More often than not, it means you have done something and she wants to talk to you so that the problem can be fixed. We enter such conversations with reluctance and, if we are honest, with prepared statements to hold up as a means of defense. The same is true in racial harmony. Whites do not want to be discovered for who they might be and have their hearts exposed, revealing what may be there. Sharp writes,

> Frustration, inhibition, resentment, shame, guilt, sorrow, anger, rage, anxiety, uncertainty—all these and countless other human emotions—are at work, underscoring the sense of fear.[85]

But if white Christians do not move beyond this, racial harmony will be stunted in the church and a fuller expression and experience of God and the gospel is forfeited within the soul. The truth of the matter is that the real problem is not finding out the nature of one's heart on this issue but the denial of sanctifying grace in dealing with what may be uncovered.

Finding that you have sin is not bad since this recognition is necessary for the grace of God to be made effectual in the soul. To find that you have tendencies towards exclusion is not bad. The tragedy would be to find these tendencies and not flee to the cross for mercy and change. The gospel is there not only to cover sin but also to empower righteousness. If fear keeps whites from the glaring light of truth, they will not engage in the battle, and racial harmony will be a mere byword.

Challenge White Privilege

Third, whites must challenge white privilege. This is the hardest hurdle to get over because it is here that we get to the root of the heart of a man. One aspect of racial division is the desire to preserve and protect what is ours. In doing this, we miss the heart of Christianity, which is to be giving and seeking to meet the needs of our brothers and sisters while holding this world and its treasures at arm's length.

There are some who would propose that all men have equal rights and abilities to progress in America. The truth of the matter, however, is that the world we live in does not operate under this notion. I do not highlight this to remove responsibility from anyone but to present the reality. Chances at progress are not equal, nor is the American Dream something that anyone and everyone can experience. Some suggest that the election of President Obama now allows young black men to dream of being anything they want to be. Dreaming is easy. Reality is not.

For every black person who achieves status and this American Dream, one hundred other blacks are judged based on what *this* man does. I remember hearing a panel discussion regarding the role of race in the hiring of head coaches in college. I remember a comment made by John Thompson, Sr., legendary coach at Georgetown University, regarding his thoughts on the future of black coaches. The question posed was whether or not coach Thompson believed his success as a coach made it easier for black coaches to be hired. It was an innocent question, but coach Thompson's remark was insightful and very instructive.

Coach Thompson stated that it was a shame that one black coach's success was deemed as the reason for other blacks being considered worthy of being hired when a white coach (and this is true for many of them) could have multiple losing seasons and still be hired very quickly by another university if he is fired. His point was clear: black coaches are judged by the success or failure of other black coaches, whereas white coaches are judged as individuals. Blacks are judged on the basis of how other blacks do while whites tend to have the privilege of being judged as individuals, regardless of what their white predecessors have done.

The path of opportunity, then, is not as equal as we might think or as the election of President Obama may cause us to assume. Again, this is not a statement that condones blame or victimology. However, it speaks to what whites have to remember as they pursue racial harmony. They must challenge this privilege.

One practical way in which this privilege can be challenged and structured is to take the money that one has by way of investments, equity, etc., and assist or put a black student through college. It is vain to speak about the lack of education among blacks and not seek to do something about it. Statistics are quoted about the percentage of blacks that drop out of school, but what can your church do to correct this? What can you do to correct this?

One cannot speak of the lack of blacks in solid theological seminaries and do nothing. There is much

166 · SHERARD BURNS

talk about the need for theological education in black churches, but, whether true or not, what can your church do about it? What can you do about this? I am the product of one such family who did not stand around and make the comments but actually did something about it.

After hearing me preach and finding out that I was going to seminary, they willingly said that they would pay for my entire seminary degree. They used their privilege and helped. Because of this, I was able not only to go to a good seminary but to learn from the best theologians in the world. You are blessed to be a blessing!

Have Courage

Fourth, whites must have courage. I have wondered over the years how and why this is such a problem in the church when so many will say all of the right things concerning racial harmony. None will say they do not want it, and none would deny that it is something that is the achievement of the cross of Christ. Yet, one need only look in homes at dinner time and observe where people hang out, live, and worship to see that, in many cases, racial harmony talk is little more than rhetoric.

For years I wanted to see this as a result of people merely not understanding the issue, but the more I have spoken with people about exclusion and racial division in the church, the more I have realized that propositional ignorance is not the only issue. What I have come to understand is that whites are not at a loss for words about racial harmony, but they don't always have the guts to do something about it! We do not have many white soldiers on this issue.

The fact is that the action required in white's remembering—the challenging of assumptions, fears, and privilege—can only take place when men and women have guts and are willing to fight with a gospel tenacity to see things as they should be and to relinquish whatever needs to be relinquished for the unity of God's people. There are plenty of words floating out in evangelicalism on the issue of racial harmony but not a lot of guts. There are a lot of stated convictions but not a lot of courage to enforce or flesh out those convictions.

Let me put this in a biblical framework. To have guts is to have faith, a great faith, to do what needs to be done to maintain the unity of the Spirit in the bond of peace. When Jesus speaks of great faith, He does so in the context of people acting and behaving in ways that challenge their current way of life. Great faith costs. Great faith is at work when after counting the cost, men and women move forward with the belief that the object of their pursuit is more valuable and worthy than anything that might be lost in the process, such as reputation, status, privilege, and wealth.

Do you have the guts to fight for this? The church needs you.

A Cross Perspective on History

This is the challenge to the white church: Will the gospel shape the contours of your engagement on the issue of race, or will you be a passive product of this culture?

If we desire to see something of a gospel impact in our churches and in our own lives, we must be people who see history from the perspective of the cross, that we might live in the present to the glory of God. No alternative, no other way, will suffice and please God. The remedy is gospel-filled people who long to express gospel realities.

At the end of the day, to pursue racial harmony means simply to pursue relationships centered around and governed by the gospel. Racial harmony is basic Christianity.

Chapter 7 Notes

_____

_____

_____

_____

_____

_____

_____

_____

_____

_____

_____

_____

_____

_____

_____

_____

_____

_____

_____

_____

_____

_____

_____

CHAPTER EIGHT

Love, Intentionality, and Humility
Radical Commitments in Pursuing Racial Harmony

It is only natural at this point to be asking, "How can this be done?" This chapter will seek to give some feet to what has already been stated. I believe that the knowledge of the gospel and the implications that attend it are sufficient to warrant our pursuit of racial harmony since the gospel is the most practical and relevant truth that man can embrace. However, there is always a need for instruction in practical application.

The call of the gospel to the pursuit of racial harmony is a radical call to live outside of ourselves. Unlike the self-help books of our day, the Bible does not point man to himself for the solution but outward to Christ, the source and the essence of our help. What is demanded in racial harmony will require the aid of heaven even in the practical things.

In this chapter, I want to offer three principles of the gospel that we must embrace if we are to see the fruit of racial harmony in our lives and churches. There must be a commitment to expressions of gospel-centered love, intentionality, and humility.

A Commitment to Gospel-Centered Love

Whenever one speaks about the need for believers to love one another, it is often confused with being emotional. This is not the essence of what I am speaking of, nor really what the Bible commands.

The dimensions of love in the Scriptures far exceed the trite and often superficial meaning it is given in the world and even within the church. The Bible speaks of love in radical, self-giving ways, and it is this kind of love that I believe is crucial in the pursuit of racial harmony. Paul instructs the church to love:

> *Therefore, be imitators of God, as beloved children. And walk in love, as Christ loved us and gave himself up for us, a fragrant offering and sacrifice to God.* — ***Ephesians 5:1-2***

The word 'imitate' is striking and practically instructive. It is the Greek word *mimētēs*, from which we get our English 'mimic.' Paul's command is grounded in the reality that believers, having been adopted into the family of God through faith in the death and resurrection of Jesus Christ, will bear the family trait of love, including love for each other.

As Christians, we are called to mimic God and to love like He loved us in Jesus when Christ sacrificially gave of Himself for the good of His bride, the church. He did this for something far greater than His comfort and ease. He did this for the glory of God, the Father. What is compelling in the picture that Paul lays out is the reality that unity necessitates death.

Our being justified, or made right with God, necessitated the death of Christ because of our sin. The death of Christ for us was not rooted in our loveliness; the exact opposite is the case. In Romans 5:8, Paul tells us that Christ died for us while we were still sinners. While we were in the midst of sin and rebellion, without any desire to please Him, Jesus died for us.

Paul's command is that we are to love one another in the same way. Crucial to our pursuit of racial harmony is a willingness to die because where there is no death—death to self, death to personal desires and preferences, death to culture—there will be no racial harmony. At the heart of the gospel is sacrificial love, a willingness to give ourselves for the sake of others and for the expression of the glory of God in and through us.

Gospel-centered love means loving the unlovely as Christ has loved us, even when we were unlovely. Sometimes other cultural norms and expressions are not what we desire or would prefer, but this has to be placed under the greater good, which is the glory of God in the harmony of the body of Christ, maintained by each member's sacrificial love.

Love, then, is not simply a feeling; it is the radical act of dying for the sake of the fuller expression of the glory of God in our churches. Perhaps we speak too much about love instead of actually loving. None would deny that we should love or that racial division is, in part, due to a lack of loving. However, we must move beyond words, clichés, and rhetoric to actual expression. If loving is a reflection of God, then it must be a demonstrated reality by His people since God did not simply love with words but actually demonstrated that love by sending His Son (John 3:16; Romans 5:8).

The Model of the Godhead

The radical call to love is further expressed in the way it comes to us and how Christ commands that it be expressed to others. The call to love others is rooted in the love expressed within the Godhead. Jesus said in John 15:9, "As the Father has loved me, so have I loved you." Then Jesus said, "This is my commandment, that you love one another as I have loved you" (John 15:12).

In this we see that the love the Father has for the Son is the same love passed on to us in the Son by way of the Holy Spirit. It is a privilege to be called to extend to others the love that has been divinely extended to us. Biblical love is not easy, and it is not always our greatest desire, because it is not based on the object of love. It is a commitment based on and flowing from the love given to us by God.

In fact, what is most radical about biblical love is that it seems to require opposition in order to be genuine. In Luke 6, we see the reality of this in Jesus' call to love:

> *Love your enemies, do good to those who hate you.... If you love those who love you, what benefit is that to you? For even sinners love those who love them.... But love your enemies ... and your reward will be great, and you will be sons of the Most High, for he is kind to the ungrateful and the evil. — **Luke 6:27, 32, 35***

Christ's call to love the unlovely and those who do us harm separates gospel-centered love from the merely selfish love of the world, which is to love those who love us.

Even more, this kind of love marks men and women as sons (and daughters) of the Most High. The way we show that we are children of the Most High is not by loving where it is easy but by loving in the midst of opposition and offense. The love we are speaking of is radical and counter-cultural.

The way this culture tends to think of love is to be loved first and then, only after that, to give love. For the believer, however, the motivation to love is our *having been loved* by Christ. Thus, the prompting of Christian love is not being loved or even the loveliness of the object but the powerful exertion of the love of God within our hearts, shed abroad by sovereign grace. In essence, in order for the love of Christ to be genuinely manifested in the lives of believers, conflict must be present.

Christians need unlovely people in their lives, whether inside the church or in the world, in order to demonstrate or prove the power of the love of Christ. Jesus loved us while we were His enemies and calls us to love our enemies in their unlovable dispositions. Love is not to be withheld until offenders come to their senses. Love is to be given in the midst of the offense, even while unkind and nasty words as well as accusations are coming your way.

These offenses must be seen as more than conflict. We must view them as opportunities given by God for us to demonstrate the worth and abundance of the love of Christ towards us by letting it overflow in kindness and love that is beyond human measure. If I did not believe this, I would have given up long ago, and so, too, would others who were in the battle long before I entered.

I think that Martin Luther King, Jr., had some understanding of this truth in desiring to be resolutely nonviolent. It was not that nonviolence was powerful in itself, but its expression was a demonstration of men and women being held by a power that transcended comfort, physical pain, slander, accusation, and retribution. When racial tension manifests itself, we should not run from it; rather, we must see it as a God-ordained opportunity to be God-like by loving the unlovely and loving when it hurts. This is the message of the cross.

This kind of sacrificial laying down of our lives for the harmony of the body of Christ is the church's greatest apologetic, or proof, of the power of the gospel. Jesus said,

A new commandment I give to you, that you love one another: just as I have loved you, you also are to love one another. By this all people will know that you are my disciples, if you have love for one another. — **John 13:34**

There is no greater defense of the faith nor a greater contradiction to it than in the expression or absence of gospel-centered love within the body of Christ. This is especially true with regard to racial division or unity.

When Jesus was told that His mother and brothers desired to speak to Him, His response was striking and instructive to us regarding racial harmony:

> *And he answered them, "Who are my mother and my brothers?" And looking about at those who sat around him, he said, "Here are my mother and my brothers! For whoever does the will of God, he is my brother and sister and mother."* — **Mark 3:33-35**

The implication is this: if we do not love a brother or sister in Christ because of his or her color or culture but love unbelievers who are of our same culture or color, not only do we not love like Christ, but we are also expressing a great hypocrisy of love.

This hypocrisy is often unseen, unheard, and unchecked because, as Volf says,

> [T]he color line has been drawn so incisively by the church itself that its proclamation of the gospel, of the brotherhood of Jew and Greek, of the bond and free, of the white and the black has sometimes the sad sound of irony, and sometimes falls upon the ears as *unconscious hypocrisy.* [emphasis added] [86]

This does not mean that we cannot have a love for non-believers. We should love unbelievers, particularly those within our own natural family. Yet, our love for those who love our Lord must supersede and be given a greater priority. This is a radically difficult truth! To love like Christ means to love in a general and a particular way. Generally speaking, the Lord loves all men (Matthew 5:44-45). However, when it comes to His bride, the church, the Scriptures declare that He loves us with an everlasting love, a love that is unto the end (John 13:1).

In *A Treatise of Christian Love* (1735), Hugh Binning explains,

> So in this a Christian should be like his Father; and there is nothing in which he resembles him more than in this, to walk in love towards all men, even our enemies.... But the particular and special current of affection will run toward the household of faith; those who are of the same descent, and family, and love.... These two in a Christian are nothing but the reflex of the love of God, and the streams issuing from it.... "As we have therefore opportunity, let us do good unto all men, especially unto them who are of the household of faith" (Galatians 6:10).[87]

To speak of the great power of Christ and the gospel as being able to redeem and change the hearts of the hardest of sinners, to speak of the radical nature in which Christ has restored relationships, to call others to embrace Christ as the great Reconciler to God, and yet, at the same time, to remain indifferent or opposed to racial harmony is a great hypocrisy and contradiction of the gospel.

John Stott put it best when he wrote,

It is simply impossible, with any shred of Christian integrity, to go on proclaiming that Jesus by his cross has abolished the old divisions and created a single new humanity of love, while at the same time we are contradicting our message by tolerating racial or social or other barriers within our church fellowship.... We need to get the failures of the church on our conscience, to feel the offense of Christ, ... to weep over the credibility gap between the church's talk and the church's walk, to repent of our readiness to excuse and even condone our failures, and to determine to do something about it. I wonder if anything is more urgent today, for the honor of Christ and the spread of the gospel, than that the church should be, and should be seen to be, what by God's purpose and Christ's achievement it already is—a single new humanity. A model of human community, a family of reconciled brothers and sisters who love their Father and love each other, the evident dwelling place of God by his Spirit. Only then will the world believe in Christ as peacemaker. Only then will God receive the glory due his name.[88]

The Supremes were right, in a sense, when they sang, "What the world needs now is love, sweet love." The love that the world needs, however, is not the love that is gushy and sentimental but that which drips and oozes gospel sacrifice.

A Commitment to Gospel-Centered Intentionality

I think one of the biggest mistakes that we can make regarding the actuality of racial harmony in our churches is thinking that it can happen with little or no effort. This is not true for any relationship, especially those that cross cultures. If the church is to be a place where the nations meet and worship the Lord Jesus Christ together,

it will be so because men and women in the church are
people given to great intentionality in crossing cultures
in their own personal relationships.

The reality of intentionality came home to me a few
years ago when I went, on two separate occasions, to
enjoy a round of golf. The first incident occurred when I
was told to join a group of three white men already on
the tee. I was happy to oblige. We all did our duties of
golf etiquette, greeting one another and stating our
names, and everyone teed off. I think it was somewhere
around the fifteenth hole that they began talking to me
and me to them. It took three plus hours before we
spoke, but the final holes were filled with chitchat and
casual conversation, with a cordial parting.

Some weeks later, I returned to the same golf course
and, again, because I was alone, was told to join a
twosome on the first tee. The men I joined on this day
were African Americans who did not know one another.
As we all hit our first shots, we began walking down the
first fairway. If you did not know us, you would have
thought that we were the best of friends and not three
guys who had just met about five minutes earlier! Why
the difference?

There may be many reasons, but one that is clear to
me is that when I played with the three white men, there
was nothing, externally speaking, that would naturally
bring us together or give us a common point of
communication. With the two black men, without even
knowing them at all, it was *as if* I knew them. I felt as if I
knew their history, their struggles, and their difficulties
because I shared something with them: we were black

men. I know what it means to be a black man in this world, and I know the struggles that attend being such. For that reason, communication was simple and easier.

Certainly there are exceptions to every rule, but, by and large, there has not been an African American that I have met with whom I did not feel a kind of familiarity. It is often commented that a black person could show up at a family reunion of a family he doesn't even know and still feel welcomed as part of that family. I have never done that, but I suspect it is true. Such familiarity and quickness of connection or communication is not so with those of another culture, however.

If I were to have a relationship with the white men I played golf with, I would have to work, as would they, to make it happen, and this is what it is going to take if racial harmony is to be a reality in the church. We do not need mere programs to attract people of a different race. What we need are more gospel soldiers, those who are willing to fight and war by wearing out their shoes, having many lunches, and embracing measures of discomfort at times, all for the sake of building bridges that can form strong and vibrant gospel relationships.

One man, concerned that the racial makeup of his church was beginning to grow increasingly white, said to his pastor, "We sure are getting a lot of white people in the church." To this the pastor said, "I guess you better start doing some black evangelism." As humorous as this may sound, it really is what a church must do if it is to be other than its dominant cultural makeup, whether black or white.

If a church is going to be intentional, its members must reach out to those whom they desire to see come to know Christ and become part of their church. Is it bad, then, to try to build a relationship with an African American or white person simply because of his or her culture? No, it is not wrong or bad. I say this for two reasons.

First, reaching out to people because they are different is the essence of intentionality, and second, intentionality is more than mere action from a distance. Some, desiring to pursue racial harmony, understand intentionality to mean little more than a mere acquaintance with people of other cultures in places where it is unavoidable. They have neighbors whom they wave at, they worship with people from other cultures, and they work with men and women of different cultures. This, however, is as far as their intentionality will go. True intentionality is more than this. Expressed in a theological, biblical framework, intentionality is incarnational.

By incarnation, I am thinking of the incarnation of the Lord Jesus Christ. God became man, being born of the virgin Mary, and took on our human form (Matthew 1:18-25). One significant aspect of the incarnation of Christ is His identifying with us by becoming man. This He did willingly so as to feel and experience our pain, thereby being a suitable savior. This is the greatest evangelistic act ever known to humankind: God became Man to win or rescue man from sin and shame. The beauty is that He *became* man.

Intentionality is the willingness not to stand at a distance and try to beckon cross-cultural relationships but to move into the realm of another person's world and existence so as to truly understand what life is like for him or her and how this person's view of the world shapes his or her understanding of life and reality. Far too often, what is conceived of by intentionality is the act of going to a place, often of a lower income bracket, doing some form of service, and then leaving while patting ourselves on the back for a job well done. This, however, is not intentionality.

Incarnational intentionality is not meeting people for the sake of their culture and color. It is going to people in order to understand their culture, the norms and values with regards to all aspects of life. The beauty in this is that it is the means of understanding one another. Martin Luther King, Jr., said that one of the reasons we are separate is because we do not communicate. I would add to that the fact that we do not communicate because we fail to express the very heart of God's act towards us: incarnation.

Instead of finding ways to be incarnational, we find reasons to flee. I have learned, personally, that the opposite of the heart that incarnates is a heart that flees. Either we are building cross-cultural relationships by going to where people are, or we are isolating ourselves so as not to be affected or impacted by them. There is no middle ground.

This idea of flight used to be termed "white flight" and signified the reality that when a neighborhood becomes increasingly minority, whites move to environments that are culturally homogeneous. White flight has been well documented and is a simple reality. I once lived in a neighborhood that experienced an influx of Asians, Africans, African Americans, and Hispanics. When this happened, "For Sale" signs became the chosen style of landscaping on my street and in the surrounding neighborhood. This is a sure sign that the "minorities" are moving in.

The idea of white flight suggests that such an attitude exists only among whites, but this is not the case. White flight could also be termed "black flight." The only problem here is that it would be politically incorrect even to suggest such a thing. The justification given by some African Americans for leaving the "hood" is that they have grown up there all of their life and now, having opportunity and resources, choose to leave in order to live in a more comfortable environment. Not only do I understand it, but it is a heart challenge for me as well.

I can understand how those who have not only grown up in impoverished neighborhoods but also lived in a time when there were little to no opportunities for African Americans would desire a better life for themselves and their families. When you reflect on history and the million ways blacks were held back and denied opportunities and good education, it seems that it would be a betrayal of all that our forefathers and mothers worked for to stay in a place that they longed to free us from so we could have better.

John Perkins is right when he speaks of our commitment to the cause of racial harmony as involving relocation. Relocation is the intentional act of moving into a neighborhood for the sake of learning its ethos, experiencing its challenges, and working to make a difference for the glory of God in identifying with others. Often we understand calls for such commitments to be made exclusively to the white community and church. However, relocation is the radical call of all who love racial harmony and desire to see communities and those in them changed by the power of the gospel.

I know of an acquaintance who was planning to go into a city to do a service project on a Saturday. He was bringing some of the men from his church and called to ask my opinion of the matter. In hearing his plan and intentions—none of which were bad—I told him that I thought that he and his men should not come. I asked if there was a plan, or intentionality, for any kind of follow-up and whether they were serious about meeting, not a day's need of the people, but the chronic and ongoing needs.

While his men would come and get their hands dirty for a day, they could go home, wash them, pat themselves on the back (with clean hands), and think no more of the continuing dirt within the area of the city they served. I recommended that if they were not ready to express an incarnational intentionality, they should partner with a ministry in the city that was. He agreed.

We cannot simply come and do projects for disadvantaged people. We must come to embrace, experience, and effectively change the ethos of the community. As with Christ, this can only happen when we incarnate and move into their realm of existence. Not all are called to leave their current neighborhoods of quiet and comfort, but all are called to contemplate ways in which they can incarnate into the life of another of a different culture for the sake of the gospel. Racial harmony will not happen if incarnation does not take place.

A Commitment to Gospel-Centered Humility

Some might say that the call of the gospel to love in the way Christ loved and the challenges involved in intentionality are daunting and seemingly impossible tasks to accomplish. To this I would heartily agree. They are difficult because they grow out of a soil that is not common to humanity. That soil is humility.

Humility is not a passive letting go of something but, rather, an active seeking of something greater than that which we release. Humility is love in action—love for God, love for people, and love for the church. While there are many references to humility in Scripture, one that is particularly helpful to our pursuit of racial harmony is found in chapter 2 of Paul's letter to the Philippian Christians.

In the context of this letter, Paul has been calling for the church to embrace and display a one-mindedness (Philippians 1:27) that is centered on the achieved realities of the gospel in their souls (Philippians 2:1-4). In doing so, he points out defective affections, "rivalry" and "conceit" (Philippians 2:3), that work against unity and should not, therefore, be expressed in our relations with one another. These terms are significant because we can trace racial division—and any other division for that matter—to the presence of such negative affections.

Paul exhorts the Philippian church and the church today to "do nothing from rivalry and conceit" (Philippians 2:3). Those who act in rivalry are those who cannot see beyond themselves. Their eyes and their hearts cannot conceive of anyone being better or more important than themselves. Rivalry came to be used metaphorically and almost exclusively of a person who persistently seeks personal advantage and gain, regardless of the effect on others.... It usually carried the idea of building oneself up by tearing someone else down.[89]

Culturally speaking, rivalry is the heart behind ethnocentrism. Those who think of their culture as being better than every other culture and treat others in such a way are acting out of a spirit of rivalry. Those who act in conceit are men and women who seek a glory that is empty and vain. To act in this way is to be self-seeking and to do and say things that bring division for the sole purpose of self-promotion and prominence.

We all, if we are honest, have acted in this way before, and there is no greater cause of racial division than this attitude. There have been, and still are, within the church ungodly desires to highlight the "evils" of a particular culture, all to prove, at least in our own minds, the prominence of our own specific culture. Whites speak of the increase of crime in the black community while blacks are constantly highlighting the negatives of police brutality as well as cultural and structural exclusion in America. To what end are these statements made?

While no one could rightly deny the reality of the statement, we must also recognize that such sentiments do not cease when we come into our churches for worship. My perceptions of whites, Christian and non-Christian, will affect my opinions of the whites I worship with if I do not fight it with the gospel. If my perception is allowed to persist unchallenged and becomes infected with rivalry and conceit, it will make my soul rotten and destroy my church! Paul, speaking to Christians who are struggling with these adverse affections, commands that they do nothing from hearts that feel in such ways.

Unity is impossible if each is out for himself, and each is promoting his own cause, each is seeking his own advantage.[90] If these vices have been part and parcel of racial division, how do we contend against such heart evils, which are present within all of us and eagerly awaiting our summons? Through the intense pursuit of humility.

After Paul gives the attitudes we are not to pursue, he supplies the positive thing to pursue: "but in humility count others more significant than yourselves" (Philippians 2:3). Paul is not saying to consider others more significant than yourself, even if they are not. No, we do not see rank-and-file sinners as more significant than ourselves, for the significance lies not in the man but in the Man, Christ, evidenced in the man or woman. This is not a socialistic gospel of seeing all things as equal regardless of morality and position in Christ. It is an appeal to see Christ in others and to make much of them.

Notice that our counting others more significant than ourselves is not humility; it is the *fruit* of humility. Paul says that we should "in humility" count others more significant. This is important to note because it means that humility is "a disposition of one's soul before it is an act." Since "rivalry" is a preoccupation with one's self and "conceit" is the desire to be glorified—preeminent above all—we can define humility as "a disposition of the soul that sees humiliation as the means to exaltation." In other words, humility is the pursuit of humiliation for the gain of exaltation.

In calling the church to humility, Paul points to the humbling (or humiliation of) Christ as the greatest example and act of humility. This is why Paul calls the church to pursue the mind of Christ (Philippians 2:5). Christ, the Son of God and God in the flesh, did not assert His divinity while on the cross but chose to suspend the use of the power of His divinity for the sake of redeeming sinners from their sin (Philippians 2:6-8).

Paul, in calling us to humility, paints before our faces the greatest of all pictures. He shows that God came down (condescended) from the splendor of penetrating glory—a glory that would instantly kill anyone who saw it in full—and stooped down into humanness, voluntarily suspending the full use of His perfections and deity in order to be and feel and experience humanness.

In painting this portrait, Paul shows that there is no greater expression of humility than God, the Creator of all things, becoming man through His descent from heaven in the Person of Christ. That the perfect Christ would take on sin and shame that was not His and experience a death that should have been ours, all for the sake of the good of His bride and the glory of the Father, is a wonder of wonders. Christ embraced humiliation but received exaltation, and in this humility, we were reconciled to God.

While we understand Christ's humility as that of *descending* from heaven, we must see our humility as an *ascending.* When we are humble and act accordingly, it feels as if we are descending, or going lower. The fact of the matter is that when we act in humility, we are ascending. Humility is living above what is natural to our human dispositions as sinners. When we are humble, we do not live below who we are; we live in the heights of heaven because of Christ's presence and power in and through us by the Holy Spirit.

The priority of humility in racial harmony is due to the fact that pursuing Christ together is not the absence of conflict. The church, like any family, will have conflict and need to be committed to resolving the conflict before it festers and causes harm to the whole of the church. Paul addressed a conflict in the Philippian church between Euodias and Syntyche by calling these women to "agree in the Lord" (Philippians 4:2). That Paul addressed this issue in such a public way shows that it had been a long-standing problem that needed to be settled, and so he mentioned the whole church in an effort to exhort church-wide support. They were to find agreement "in the Lord."

In other words, the disagreement was such that one or both had departed from the centrality of Christ in their affections and from the disposition of humility. Long-standing conflict is sometimes owing to one or both sides believing themselves to be right and holding on until the other side recognizes this. In calling these women to agree in the Lord, Paul was calling them to remember the example of Christ and the exhortation to kill pride by counting others as more significant than their own personal interests. He called them to move from where they were, their personal positions, to the center and there, in the nearness of Christ (Philippians 4:5), to agree. This takes humility.

The divisions in America have been long-standing divisions, and when and because they were allowed to continue, they have become cemented realities. The racial divisions and exclusion within the church are disagreements that must be challenged to move from their corners into the middle of the ring and not fight but, instead, find Christ in the matter. The inability to move, give up, and count others more significant than ourselves is a defiant expression of pride.

While all pride can be seen as rebellion, this kind of pride is defiant rebellion because, as lovers of the humble Christ, we know it is wrong to choose not to move despite our knowledge of the example He instructs us to follow. Should we be so proud when our Christ has been so humble?

The Imperative Grounded in Indicatives

As we pursue the cause of racial harmony and desire to reflect something of the character of our Lord Jesus Christ, the beauty of the gospel is this: we are not called to accomplish something in our own strength and power.

Augustine is quoted as saying to God, "Command what You will, but supply what You command." This is exactly what God has done in the Lord Jesus Christ. Imperatives are commands that are given by God to the church to guide how we live and conduct ourselves in the church and the world. These commands of God are not empty commands. His call is not a bare call, empty and void of enabling power to achieve and live out what He commands.

God is not the distant One who issues a call and then stands back to see what we can make of it or whether or not we can actually do it. The gospel has accomplished much more than that. Paul highlights this fact beautifully, saying,

> Therefore, my beloved, as you have always obeyed, so now, not only as in my presence but much more in my absence, work out your own salvation with fear and trembling ... —
> **Philippians 2:12**

We are commanded to "work out" our salvation in the context of the local church to which we belong; but, again, this is no empty command.

Paul is not advocating a works-oriented salvation. He highlights the powerful influence of God in, over, and through the work by adding these words: "for it is God who works in you, both to will and to work for his good pleasure" (Philippians 2:13). The God who commanded us through Paul is the same God who works in and through us that which He commands. This is the beauty of the gospel and the only hope for racial harmony in the church.

It is not a call to love, to be intentional, and to be humble in our own strength; these things are beyond our natural desires. By the grace of God, in the power of the gospel applied to our souls by the Holy Spirit, we have Christ in us, and in Christ, we are enabled to demonstrate commitment to gospel-centered love, intentionality, and humility.

The reality that all of the power of heaven resides within us, enabling us to obey the commands of the Lord, gives us the right to say with Paul, "I can do all things through him who strengthens me" (Philippians 4:13). The pursuit of racial harmony is the cultivation of the soul that expresses the beauty of Christ, having love, intentionality, and humility as its chief aim within the church and in the world. This is a disposition that cannot be achieved except by the power of the Holy Spirit within us. If racial harmony is to be a reality within our churches, it must first be a passion within our souls. When this happens, all of hell and its production of racial exclusion and division will not be able to contend.

Chapter 8 Notes

CONCLUSION

New Eyes, New Hearts

It is my hope that Christ will use the pages of this book to do the necessary surgery on all of our hearts to begin the pilgrimage towards racial harmony. We should know that it is never a done deal until Christ takes us home, but we must ever look to Him to be making us more and more like Him so that we might love more and more like He loves. He alone is our hope.

May our churches battle against cultural complicity on this issue of exclusion and may we, as one man said in a conference, become cycle breakers and legacy makers. Let us learn how to talk with and not simply talk at one another. Let us not turn a blind eye or a deaf ear to injustice, exclusion, and suffering, knowing that the God of the universe, our Father in heaven, sees and hears all.

Let us not allow our lives, attitudes, and pursuits to remain prisoners of the past, no matter how devastating or shameful that past was, knowing that all are guilty of the sin for which Christ died and all who believe are recipients of the grace and forgiveness Christ paid so dearly to make available to us.

Let us break the cycles of cultural influence and build legacies of racial harmony rooted in the gospel, setting our sights and our hearts on the fulfillment of the sovereign God's divine plan for His church of many peoples united in the one Person of Christ.

With the psalmist, we say,

> *I lift up my eyes to the hills. From where does my help come? My help comes from the LORD, who made heaven and earth.* — **Psalm 121:1-2**

Amen, and let it be so.

REFERENCES

Notes

1. "Racism." *Webster's New World Dictionary of the American Language*: *College Edition*. Cleveland and New York: The World Publishing Company, 1962.
2. D'Souza, Dinesh. *The End of Racism*. New York: Free Press Paperbacks, 1995.
3. Bell, Derrick. *Faces at the Bottom of the Well*: *The Permanence of Racism*. New York: Basic Books, 1992.
4. Sowell, Thomas. *Race and Culture*: *A World View*. New York: Basic Books, 1994. p. 154.
5. Carson, D. A. *Love in Hard Places*. Wheaton, IL: Crossway Books, 2002. p. 88.
6. Volf, Miroslav. *Exclusion and Embrace: A Theological Exploration of Identity, Otherness and Reconciliation*. Nashville: Abingdon Press, 1996.
7. Volf, Miroslav. *Exclusion and Embrace: A Theological Exploration of Identity, Otherness*

and Reconciliation. Nashville: Abingdon Press, 1996. p. 75.

8. Volf, Miroslav. *Exclusion and Embrace: A Theological Exploration of Identity, Otherness and Reconciliation.* Nashville: Abingdon Press, 1996. p. 75.

9. Volf, Miroslav. *Exclusion and Embrace: A Theological Exploration of Identity, Otherness and Reconciliation.* Nashville: Abingdon Press, 1996. p. 75.

10. Emerson, Michael O., and Christian Smith. *Divided by Faith: Evangelical Religion and the Problem of Race in America.* New York: Oxford University Press, 2000. p. 7.

11. Emerson, Michael O., and Christian Smith. *Divided by Faith: Evangelical Religion and the Problem of Race in America.* New York: Oxford University Press, 2000. p. 22.

12. Volf, Miroslav. *Exclusion and Embrace: A Theological Exploration of Identity, Otherness and Reconciliation.* Nashville: Abingdon Press, 1996. p. 75.

13. Volf, Miroslav. *Exclusion and Embrace: A Theological Exploration of Identity, Otherness and Reconciliation.* Nashville: Abingdon Press, 1996. p. 75.

14. Oden, Thomas C. *How Africa Shaped the Christian Mind: Rediscovering the African Seedbed of Western Christianity.* Downers Grove, IL: InterVarsity Press, 2007.

15. Volf, Miroslav. *Exclusion and Embrace: A Theological Exploration of Identity, Otherness and Reconciliation.* Nashville: Abingdon Press, 1996. p. 40.

16. Carson, D. A. *Love in Hard Places.* Wheaton, IL: Crossway Books, 2002. p. 91.

17. Harris, Murray J. *Slaves of Christ: A New Testament Metaphor for Total Devotion to Christ.* Downers Grove, IL: InterVarsity Press, 1999. p. 54.

18. Dabney, Robert L. *A Defense of Virginia, and Through Her, of the South, in Recent and Pending Contests Against the Sectional Party.* 1867. Harrisonburg, VA: Sprinkle Publications, 1991. p. 157.

19. Wilson, Doug. *Black and Tan: Essays and Excursions on Slavery, Culture War and Scripture in America.* Moscow, ID: Canon Press, 2005. p. 41.

20. Wilson, Doug. *Black and Tan: Essays and Excursions on Slavery, Culture War and Scripture in America.* Moscow, ID: Canon Press, 2005. p. 42.

21. (Christianity and Slavery, p. 37)

22. Holifield, E. Brooks. *Theology in America: Christian Thought from the Age of the Puritans to the Civil War.* New Haven and London: Yale University Press, 2003. p. 496.

23. Burns, Sherard. "Trusting the Theology of a Slave Owner." *A God Entranced Vision of All Things: The Legacy of Jonathan Edwards.* Ed.

John Piper and Justin Taylor. Wheaton, Illinois: Crossway Books, 2004. p. 145-71.

24. p. 149

25. p. 149

26. Emerson, Michael O., and Christian Smith. *Divided by Faith: Evangelical Religion and the Problem of Race in America.* New York: Oxford University Press, 2000. p. 25.

27. Sweet, William Warren. *The Story of Religion in America.* New York: Harper & Brothers Publishers, 1950. p. 171.

28. Wheatley, Phillis. "On the Death of the Rev. Mr. George Whitefield. 1770." *Phillis Wheatley: Complete Writings.* Ed. Vincent Carretta. New York: Penguin Books, 2001. p. 15.

29. Saillant, John. "Wipe away All Tears from Their Eyes: John Murrant's Theology in the Black Atlantic." *Journal of Millennial Studies* 1.2 (Winter 1999).

30. Emerson, Michael O., and Christian Smith. *Divided by Faith: Evangelical Religion and the Problem of Race in America.* New York: Oxford University Press, 2000. p. 26.

31. Emerson, Michael O., and Christian Smith. *Divided by Faith: Evangelical Religion and the Problem of Race in America.* New York: Oxford University Press, 2000. p. 26.

32. Emerson, Michael O., and Christian Smith. *Divided by Faith: Evangelical Religion and the Problem of Race in America.* New York: Oxford University Press, 2000. p. 26.

33. Peart, Norman Anthony. *Separate No More: Understanding and Developing Racial Reconciliation in Your Church.* Grand Rapids, MI: Baker, 2000. p. 27.
34. Dallimore, Arnold. *George Whitefield: The Life and Times of the Great Evangelist of the 18th-Century Revival.* 2 vols. Carlisle, PA: Banner of Truth, 2001. Vol. 1, p. 495.
35. Hardman, Keith J. *Issues in American History: Primary Sources with Introductions.* Grand Rapids, MI: Baker, 1993. p. 66.
36. Dallimore, Arnold. *George Whitefield: The Life and Times of the Great Evangelist of the 18th-Century Revival.* 2 vols. Carlisle, PA: Banner of Truth, 2001. Vol. 2, p. 219.
37. Dallimore, Arnold. *George Whitefield: The Life and Times of the Great Evangelist of the 18th-Century Revival.* 2 vols. Carlisle, PA: Banner of Truth, 2001. Vol. 2, p. 219.
38. Dallimore, Arnold. *George Whitefield: The Life and Times of the Great Evangelist of the 18th-Century Revival.* 2 vols. Carlisle, PA: Banner of Truth, 2001. Vol. 2, p. 219.
39. Dallimore, Arnold. *George Whitefield: The Life and Times of the Great Evangelist of the 18th-Century Revival.* 2 vols. Carlisle, PA: Banner of Truth, 2001. Vol. 2, p. 521.
40. Dabney, Robert L. *A Defense of Virginia, and Through Her, of the South, in Recent and Pending Contests Against the Sectional Party.*

1867. Harrisonburg, VA: Sprinkle Publications, 1991. p. 6.

41. Wells, David. *Reformed Theology in America: A History of Its Development*. Grand Rapids, MI: Baker, 1998. p. 217.

42. Dabney, Robert L. *A Defense of Virginia, and Through Her, of the South, in Recent and Pending Contests Against the Sectional Party*. 1867. Harrisonburg, VA: Sprinkle Publications, 1991. p. 7.

43. Wilson, Doug. *Black and Tan: Essays and Excursions on Slavery, Culture War and Scripture in America*. Moscow, ID: Canon Press, 2005. p. 88.

44. Ellis, Carl. *Free at Last: The Gospel in the African American Experience*. Downers Grove, IL: Intervarsity Press, 1996. p. 20.

45. Ellis, Carl. *Free at Last: The Gospel in the African American Experience*. Downers Grove, IL: Intervarsity Press, 1996. p. 214.

46. Wells, David. *Reformed Theology in America: A History of Its Development*. Grand Rapids, MI: Baker, 1998. p. 217.

47. Noll, Mark A. *America's God: From Jonathan Edwards to Abraham Lincoln*. New York: Oxford University Press, 2002. p. 396.

48. Dallimore, Arnold. *George Whitefield: The Life and Times of the Great Evangelist of the 18th-Century Revival*. 2 vols. Carlisle, PA: Banner of Truth, 2001. Vol. 2, p. 368.

49. Peart, Norman Anthony. *Separate No More: Understanding and Developing Racial Reconciliation in Your Church.* Grand Rapids, MI: Baker, 2000. p. 38-39.

50. Norrell, Robert J. *The House I Live In: Race in the American Century.* New York: Oxford University Press, 2005.

51. Norrell, Robert J. *The House I Live In: Race in the American Century.* New York: Oxford University Press, 2005. p. 8-9.

52. Saillant, John. *Black Puritan, Black Republican: The Life and Thought of Lemuel Haynes, 1753–1833.* New York: Oxford University Press, 2003. p. 100-101.

53. D'Souza, Dinesh. *The End of Racism.* New York: Free Press Paperbacks, 1995.

54. D'Souza, Dinesh. *The End of Racism.* New York: Free Press Paperbacks, 1995.

55. D'Souza, Dinesh. *The End of Racism.* New York: Free Press Paperbacks, 1995.

56. Carroll, Vincent, and David Shiftlett. *Christianity on Trial: Arguments Against Anti-Religious Bigotry.* San Francisco: Encounter Books, 2002. p. 31.

57. Carroll, Vincent, and David Shiftlett. *Christianity on Trial: Arguments Against Anti-Religious Bigotry.* San Francisco: Encounter Books, 2002. p. 31.

58. Holifield, E. Brooks. *Theology in America: Christian Thought from the Age of the Puritans*

to the Civil War. New Haven and London: Yale University Press, 2003. p. 494.

59. Volf, Miroslav. *Exclusion and Embrace: A Theological Exploration of Identity, Otherness and Reconciliation*. Nashville: Abingdon Press, 1996. p. 36.

60. Emerson, Michael O., and Christian Smith. *Divided by Faith: Evangelical Religion and the Problem of Race in America*. New York: Oxford University Press, 2000. p. 9.

61. Frame, John. *The Doctrine of God*. Phillipsburg, NJ: Presbyterian and Reformed Publishing, 2001. p. 81.

62. Rainey, Dennis. *Weekend to Remember: Get Away to Come Together*. Little Rock, AZ: 2011. p. 12.

63. Sharp, Douglas R. *No Partiality: The Idolatry of Race and the New Humanity*. Downers Grove, IL: InterVarsity Press, 2002. p. 240.

64. Frame, John. *The Doctrine of the Knowledge of God*. Phillipsburg, NJ: Presbyterian and Reformed Publishing, 1987. p. 76.

65. Packer, James I. "What is Evangelism?" *Theological Perspectives on Church Growth*. Ed. Harvie M. Conn. Phillipsburg, NJ: Presbyterian and Reformed Publishing, 1976. p. 91.

66. Piper, John. "The Reformed Faith and Racial Harmony." 19 Jan. 2003. Sermon. www.Desiringgod.org.

67. p. 31

68. Volf, Miroslav. *Exclusion and Embrace: A Theological Exploration of Identity, Otherness, and Reconciliation.* Nashville, TN: Abingdon Press, 1996. p. 38.
69. Volf, Miroslav. *Exclusion and Embrace: A Theological Exploration of Identity, Otherness, and Reconciliation.* Nashville, TN: Abingdon Press, 1996. p. 40.
70. O'Brien, Peter. "The Letter to the Ephesians." *The Pillar New Testament Commentary.* Ed. D. A. Carson. Grand Rapids, MI: Eerdmans, 1999. p. 245.
71. Perry, Dwight. "Developing a Biblical Theology of Racial Reconciliation." *Building Unity in the Church of the New Millennium.* Ed. Dwight Perry. Chicago, IL: Moody Press, 2002. p. 39.
72. Emerson, Michael O., and Christian Smith. *Divided by Faith: Evangelical Religion and the Problem of Race in America.* New York: Oxford University Press, 2000. p. 117.
73. MacArthur, John. *Why One Way? Defending an Exclusive Claim in an Inclusive World.* Nashville: W. Publishing Group, 2002. p. 13.
74. Wells, David. *Above All Earthly Pow'rs: Christ in a Postmodern World.* Grand Rapids: Eerdmans, 2005. p. 7.
75. Hays, J. Daniel. *From Every People and Nation: A Biblical Theology of Race.* Ed. D. A. Carson. Downers Grove, IL: InterVarsity Press, 2003. p. 191.

76. Steele, Shelby. *A Dream Deferred: The Second Betrayal of Black Freedom in America*. New York: Harper Collins, 1998. p. 11.

77. Chenu, Bruno. *The Trouble I've Seen: The Big Book of Negro Spirituals*. Valley Forge, PA: Judson Press, 2003.

78. Carson, D. A. *Love in Hard Places*. Wheaton, IL: Crossway, 2002. p. 101-102.

79. Volf, Miroslav. *Exclusion and Embrace: A Theological Exploration of Identity, Otherness, and Reconciliation*. Nashville, TN: Abingdon Press, 1996. p. 123.

80. Volf, Miroslav. *Exclusion and Embrace: A Theological Exploration of Identity, Otherness, and Reconciliation*. Nashville, TN: Abingdon Press, 1996. p. 125.

81. Perry, Dwight. "Developing a Biblical Theology of Racial Reconciliation: How Do Institutions Perpetuate Racism?" *Building Unity in the Church of the New Millennium*. Ed. Dwight Perry. Chicago, IL: Moody Press, 2002. p. 35.

82. Sharp, Douglas R. *No Partiality: The Idolatry of Race and the New Humanity*. Downers Grove, IL: InterVarsity Press, 2002. p. 24.

83. Sharp, Douglas R. *No Partiality: The Idolatry of Race and the New Humanity*. Downers Grove, IL: InterVarsity Press, 2002. p. 24.

84. Sharp, Douglas R. *No Partiality: The Idolatry of Race and the New Humanity*. Downers Grove, IL: InterVarsity Press, 2002. p. 22.

85. Sharp, Douglas R. *No Partiality: The Idolatry of Race and the New Humanity.* Downers Grove, IL: InterVarsity Press, 2002. p. 23.
86. Volf, Miroslav. *Exclusion and Embrace: A Theological Exploration of Identity, Otherness and Reconciliation.* Nashville: Abingdon Press, 1996. p. 36.
87. Binning, Hugh. *Christian Love.* Carlisle, PA: Banner of Truth, 2004. p. 6-7.
88. Stott, John.
89. MacArthur, John. *Philippians.* Chicago, IL: Moody Press, 2001. Logos Bible Software.
90. Hawthorne, Gerald. "Philippians." *Word Biblical Commentary.* Ed. Bruce Metzger. Nashville, TN: Thomas Nelson, 1983. p. 68.

About the Author

Sherard Burns has been speaking, writing and preaching on the issue
of racial unity in the church for over 25 years to those who are
challenged by it and those who embrace it. He conducts seminars as

well as leadership training that equip churches and organizations to build vision and practical application.

He has served as pastor in white and black churches and his seminar, "Racial Harmony and the Gospel"—both nationally and internationally—has equipped countless individuals in dozens of churches to make an impact in this area. His educational background in biblical and theological studies has provided him with insight into how doctrine shapes and should impact every aspect of church life and culture as well as the broader culture in general.

Burns spreads his Christ-centered message of racial unity through his "Racial harmony and the Gospel" workshops, and he also serves as the president of the Multi-cultural Pastors Network in Miami, Florida—a network of pastors committed to building cross-cultural fellowship for the glory of Christ. Aside from these responsibilities he enjoys reading, writing, blogging and golf. You can learn more about Sherard and his ministry at sherardkburns.com.

About Sermon To Book

SermonToBook.com began with a simple belief: that sermons should be touching lives, *not* collecting dust. That's why we turn sermons into high-quality books that are accessible to people all over the globe.

Turning your sermon series into a book exposes more people to God's Word, better equips you for counseling, accelerates future sermon prep, adds credibility to your ministry, and even helps make ends meet during tight times.

John 21:25 tells us that the world itself couldn't contain the books that would be written about the work of Jesus Christ. Our mission is to try anyway. Because, in Heaven, there will no longer be a need for sermons or books. Our time is now.

If God so leads you, we'd love to work with you on your sermon or sermon series.

Visit www.sermontobook.com to learn more.

72954377R00120

Made in the USA
Columbia, SC
03 July 2017